To my children, Will, Jess, Becky and Nick, and Shannon, Jamie, and Fede, and their children, who can make that! — M.W.

Text © 2014 Mary Wallace

This book contains material that has previously appeared in *I Can Make That!* © 2002, *I Can Make Costumes* © 1996, *I Can Make Puppets* © 1994, *I Can Make Nature Crafts* © 1996, *I Can Make Toys* © 1994, *I Can Make Games* © 1995.

The crafts in this book have been tested and are safe when conducted as instructed. The author and publisher accept no responsibility for any damage caused or sustained by the use or misuse of ideas or material featured in the crafts in *I Can Make That!*

Owlkids Books acknowledges the financial support of the Canada Council for the Arts, the Ontario Arts Council, the Government of Canada through the Canada Book Fund (CBF) and the Government of Ontario through the Ontario Media Development Corporation's Book Initiative for our publishing activities.

Published in Canada by
Owlkids Books Inc.
10 Lower Spadina Avenue
Toronto, ON M5V 2Z2

Published in the United States by
Owlkids Books Inc.
1700 Fourth Street
Berkeley, CA 94710

Library and Archives Canada Cataloguing in Publication

Wallace, Mary, 1950-, author   I can make that! : fantastic crafts for kids / Mary Wallace.
-- Revised edition

Includes index. ISBN 978-1-926973-97-5 (bound)

     1. Handicraft--Juvenile literature. I. Title.

TT160.W354 2014   j745.5   C2013-904510-4

Library of Congress Control Number: 2013949441

Design: Barb Kelly

Photos: Melissa Peretti—Cover, 3 (hands), 21, 25 (head wreath), 33 (color rings), 35, 54–55, 58 (grouping and finger), 62 (audience), 64 (kids on floor), 130 and back cover (girl and club). All other photos © Mary Wallace

Manufactured in Shenzhen, China, in November 2013, by C&C Joint Printing Co.
Job #HN5511

A   B   C   D   E   F

Publisher of Chirp, chickaDEE and OWL
www.owlkidsbooks.com

I Can Make That!

Fantastic Crafts for Kids!

Mary Wallace

Owl kids

Contents

46

17

Roarrrr!

84

101

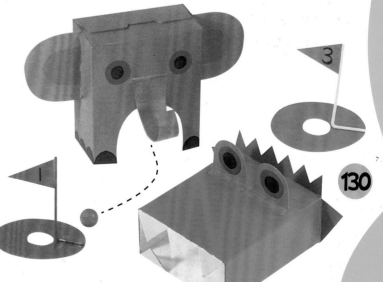

119

130

Getting Started

This book is filled with amazing crafts you can make. It's easy. It's fun. And you'll find most of what you need around your home and outside.

Check out the index on page 150 to see what you can make with the materials you have on hand.

The craft ideas can also be used to spark your imagination and start you thinking about how to invent your own creations.

Use lots of color to make your crafts bright. Before you begin, cover your table with newspaper or plastic to catch any drips. And remember, always get permission to use what you find, and take only what you need.

If you don't have the materials suggested, you can always use something different and

decorate as you like

Here are some more tips on decorating your crafts.

Colored Tape and Stickers

are easy to use, and they don't make any mess.

White Glue
is safe and cleans up easily.

• Use it to stick on colored paper and other decorations.

• Get the kind that dries clear.

• Let dry for 24 hours before playing.

• Mix half glue and half water and brush over dried paint for a glossy, smear-proof finish.

Markers and Crayons

are an inexpensive way to add color.

- Use them to add details.
- Use mostly for small sections (might smudge if used to cover large pieces).

Tempera Paint

is inexpensive and easy to use.

- Use it on paper, cardboard, and wood.
- Wash it out with water.
- Mix with a few drops of liquid soap to make it stick to a waxy surface.
- Finish with white glue to keep it from rubbing off (see tips on previous page).

Acrylic Paint

(or fabric paint) comes in bright colors and is waterproof once it dries.

- Use it on almost any surface.
- Clean up with water while paint is still wet.
- Clean up fast—does NOT wash out of brushes, clothing, or rugs when dry.
- Use with a toothpick or fabric paint marker for small details.

Stapling Tip:

When stapling rings to fit around head, cover the inside surface with tape to keep staples from poking or catching.

These are some of the ways the projects in this book have been decorated. And your crafts can be even more special if you use ideas of your own.

Be silly. Be daring. Be creative. Have fun!

Let's Make Costumes

Superheroes

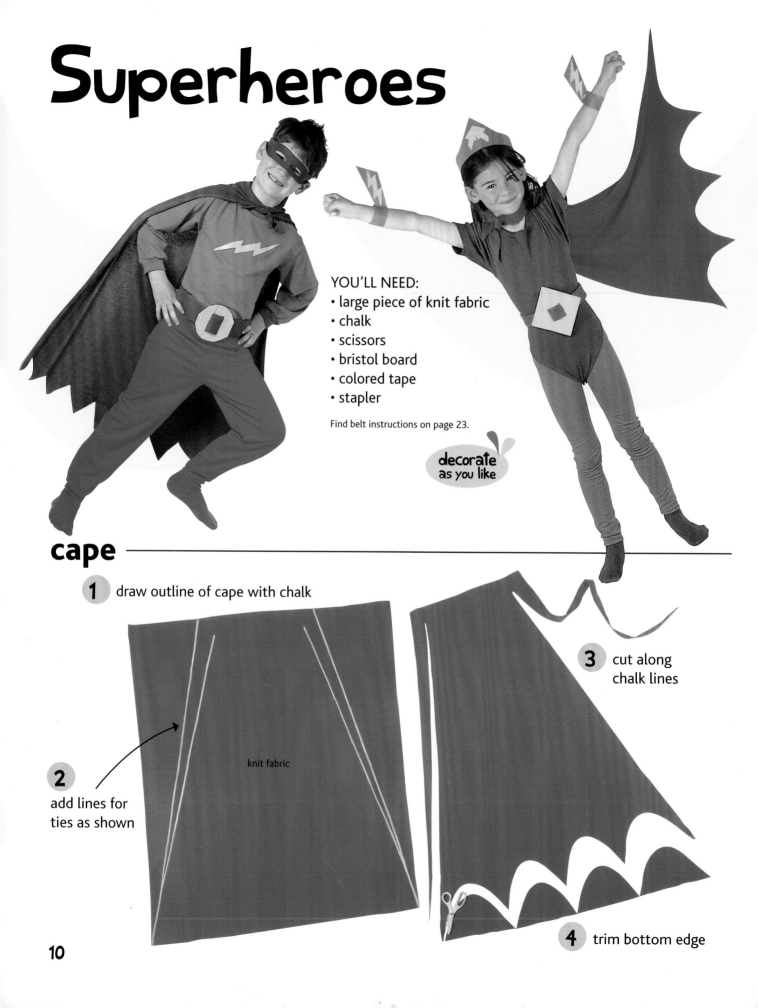

YOU'LL NEED:
- large piece of knit fabric
- chalk
- scissors
- bristol board
- colored tape
- stapler

Find belt instructions on page 23.

decorate as you like

cape

1 draw outline of cape with chalk

2 add lines for ties as shown

knit fabric

3 cut along chalk lines

4 trim bottom edge

mask

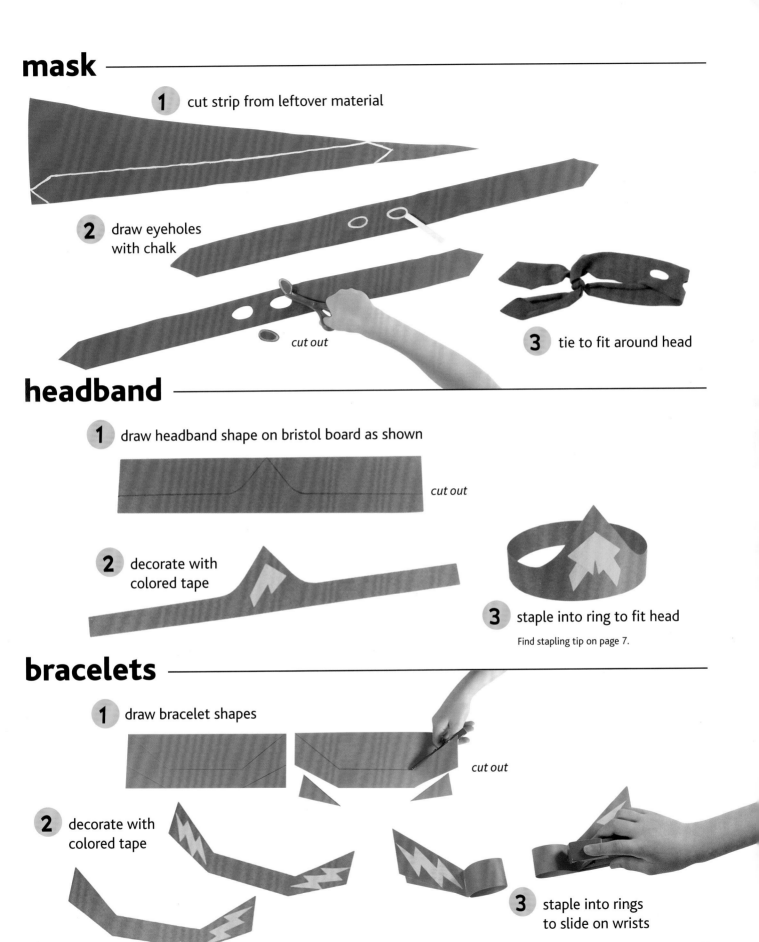

1 cut strip from leftover material

2 draw eyeholes with chalk

cut out

3 tie to fit around head

headband

1 draw headband shape on bristol board as shown

cut out

2 decorate with colored tape

3 staple into ring to fit head

Find stapling tip on page 7.

bracelets

1 draw bracelet shapes

cut out

2 decorate with colored tape

3 staple into rings to slide on wrists

Star Explorer

spaceship

YOU'LL NEED:
- cardboard box
- scissors
- bristol board
- hole punch
- metal paper fasteners
- markers
- 2 chairs
- pillows
- tape

1 cut off box flaps and up 2 sides

cut
cut

2 cut out dials and punch holes, then attach dials to control panel with paper fasteners

fold
control panel

decorate as you like

3 place box over 1 chair

4 place 2 chairs together

5 stack pillows between chair legs

6 cut out tail and nose pieces from bristol board and tape onto chairs

tail
fold
nose
tail

helmet

YOU'LL NEED:
- container to fit over head*
- scissors
- aluminum foil
- tape

* Ask for a carton, like the one shown, at an ice cream shop.

ASK FOR ADULT HELP

1 cut slits for shoulders

2 cut viewing hole

3 cover with aluminum foil

4 fold edges in and secure with tape

space alien

YOU'LL NEED:
- bristol board
- scissors
- stapler
- tape

1 cut 3 strips of bristol board

top pieces

head strap

measure to fit around head

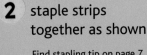

2 staple strips together as shown

Find stapling tip on page 7.

3 cut eye shape and other pieces from bristol board and staple them on

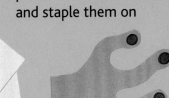

Dress-up Zoo

MOUSE

YOU'LL NEED:
- bristol board
- stapler
- pencil
- colored paper
- scissors
- clear tape
- hole punch
- yarn
- rope
- large safety pin

ears

1 staple bristol board strip into ring to fit head

2 draw ears on paper

cut out

3 staple ears to ring

Find stapling tip on page 7.

nose

1 cut paper as shown

2 roll into cone and tape

3 punch 2 holes

reinforce holes with tape

4 cut 2 pieces of yarn to fit around head

5 thread yarn through holes and knot

6 tape on yarn whiskers

tail

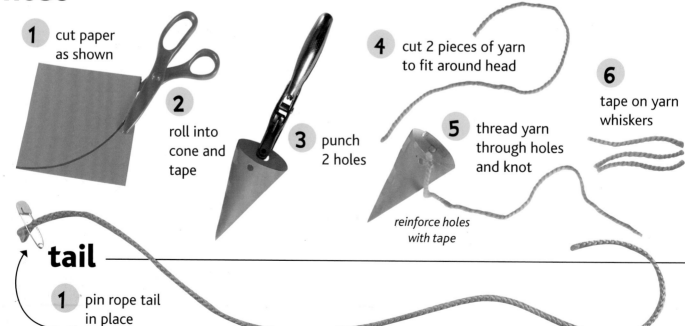

1 pin rope tail in place

RABBIT

YOU'LL NEED:
- bristol board
- stapler
- pencil
- scissors
- 3 plastic bags
- twist tie
- large safety pin
- socks
- fabric paint

ears

1 staple bristol board strip into ring to fit head

2 draw ears on bristol board

cut out

3 staple ears to ring

Find stapling tip on page 7.

tail

1 cut tops and bottoms off bags

2 pile them on top of each other

3 twist in the middle and fasten with a twist tie

gather

paws

1 paint paw details on socks, then slip onto hands

fluff tail and pin it in place

15

REINDEER

YOU'LL NEED:
• bristol board
• stapler
• pencil
• colored paper
• scissors

1 staple bristol board strip into ring to fit head

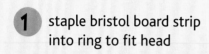

staple

2 trace hands and wrists onto paper and cut out

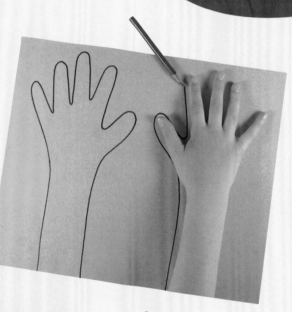

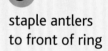

3 staple antlers to front of ring

4 draw ears on paper and cut out

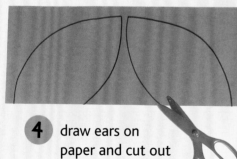

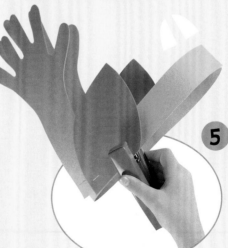

5 staple ears to sides of ring

Find stapling tip on page 7.

16

TIGER

YOU'LL NEED:
- bristol board
- pencil
- scissors
- stapler
- hole punch
- yarn
- old sweatsuit
- acrylic paint and brush
- newspapers
- stocking
- polyester stuffing
- large safety pin

ASK FOR ADULT HELP

ears

1 cut bristol board strip to fit over top of head

2 draw ears and cut out

3 staple ears to strip

4 punch 2 holes, then thread yarn through and knot

fold up ears

body

1 paint stripes on sweatsuit and let dry before wearing

tail

1 stuff tail and paint stripes, let dry, then pin in place

17

Face Paint Fun

ASK FOR ADULT HELP

YOU'LL NEED:
- 1 spoonful of shortening
- 2 spoonfuls of cornstarch
- bowl
- spoon
- ice-cube tray
- food coloring
- paintbrush
- warm water

1 mix shortening and cornstarch in bowl

2 put mixture in ice-cube tray, using 1 section for each color

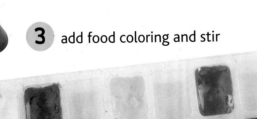

3 add food coloring and stir

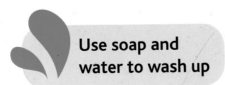

Use soap and water to wash up

mix to get the color you want

blue	+ red	= purple
blue	+ yellow	= green
yellow	+ red	= orange
yellow+red+blue		= black

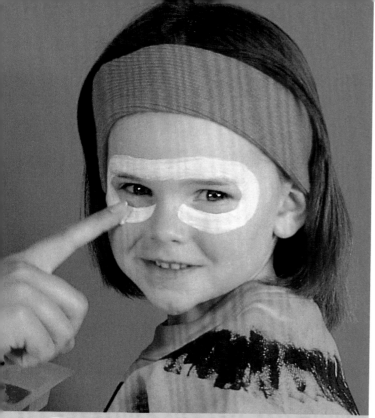

1 dip finger in warm water, then in face paint, and apply (be careful near eyes)

2 paint orange and white with your finger

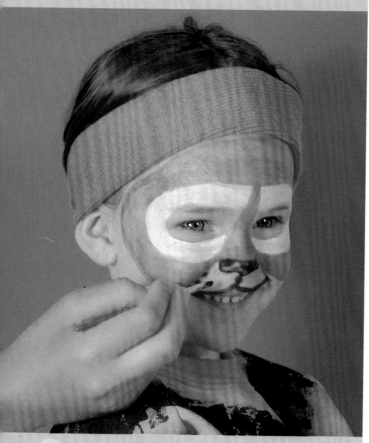

3 add details with a paintbrush dipped in warm water and black paint

Starry Eyes

ASK FOR ADULT HELP

YOU'LL NEED:
- egg carton
- scissors
- hole punch
- pipe cleaners
- shiny paper
- sequins
- white glue

1 cut 2 cups

2 trim as shown

3 cut eyeholes

4 punch holes at both sides

5 use pipe cleaner to fasten in center

twist the ends

6 put pipe cleaners through side holes

7 bend ends to fit over ears

twist the ends

decorate as you like

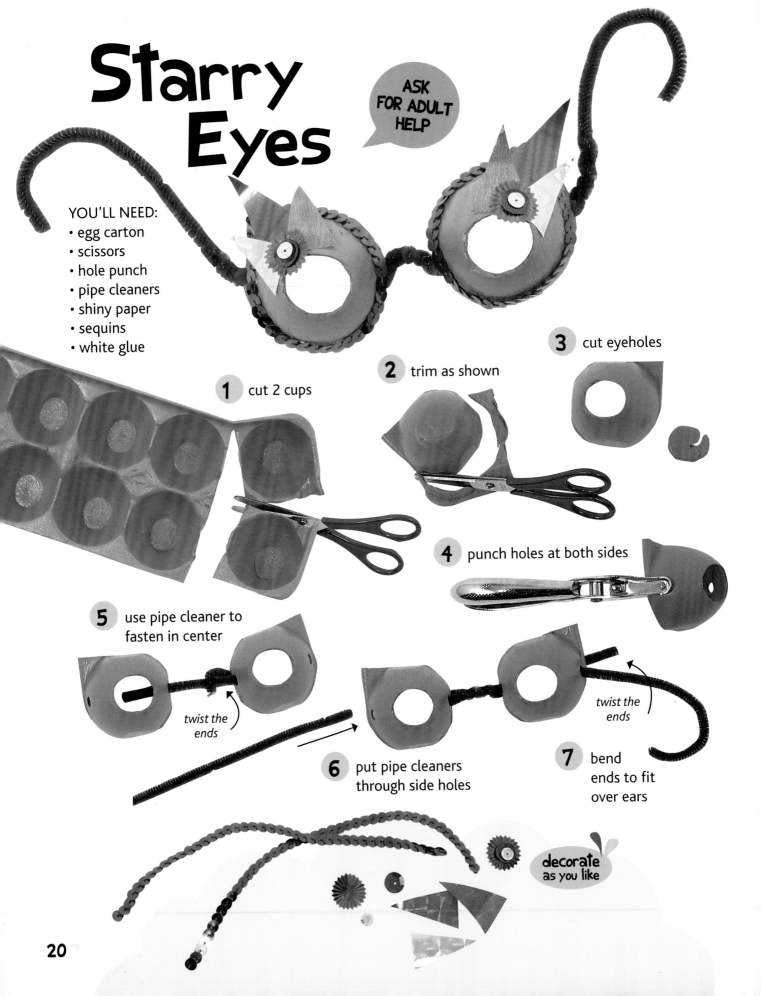

Bag Vest

YOU'LL NEED:
- large brown paper bag
- crayons
- scissors

1 crinkle paper bag
and smooth it out

*repeat until
bag is soft*

2 draw and cut out
arm and neck holes

decorate
as you like

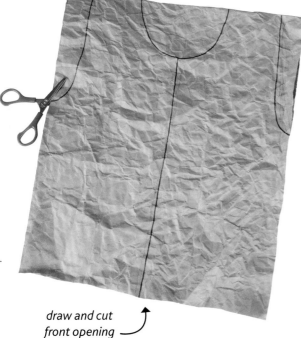

*draw and cut
front opening*

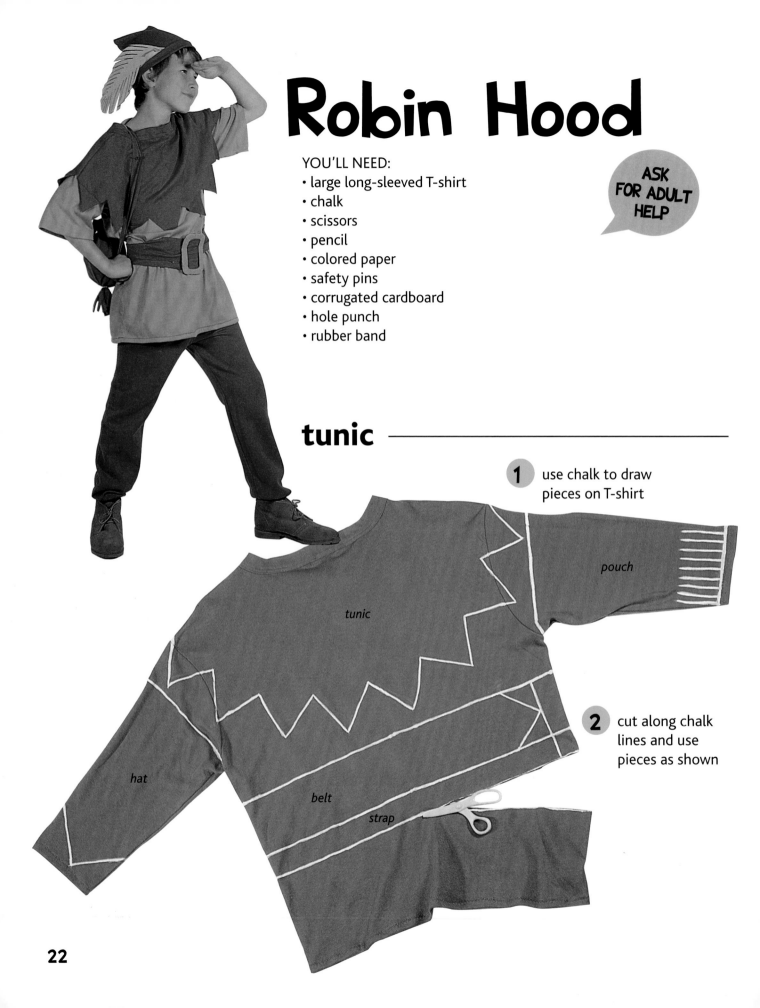

Robin Hood

YOU'LL NEED:
- large long-sleeved T-shirt
- chalk
- scissors
- pencil
- colored paper
- safety pins
- corrugated cardboard
- hole punch
- rubber band

ASK FOR ADULT HELP

tunic

1 use chalk to draw pieces on T-shirt

2 cut along chalk lines and use pieces as shown

pouch

tunic

hat

belt

strap

hat

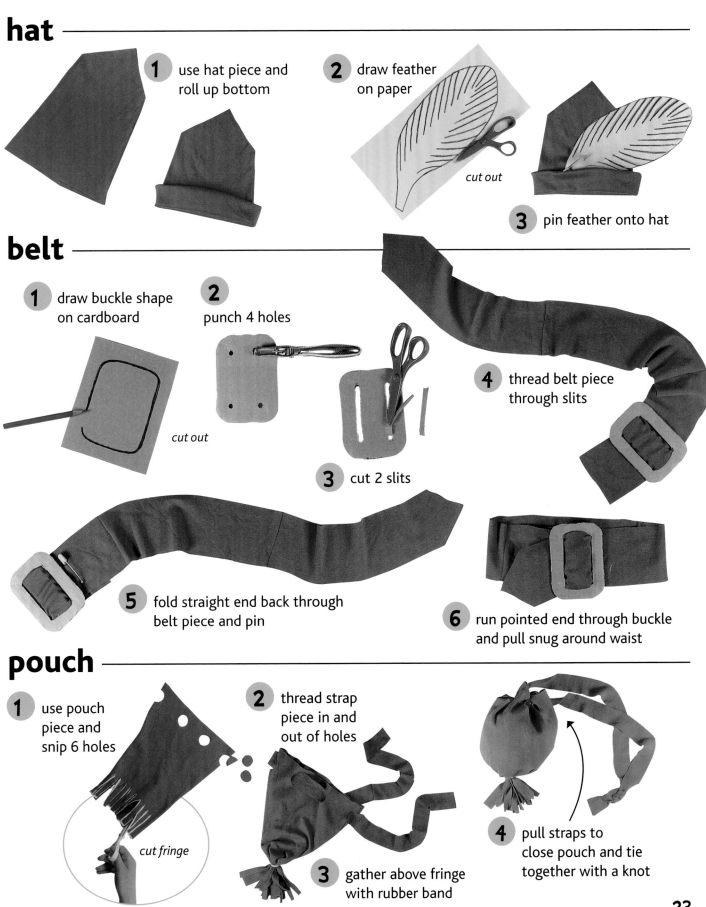

1 use hat piece and roll up bottom

2 draw feather on paper

cut out

3 pin feather onto hat

belt

1 draw buckle shape on cardboard

cut out

2 punch 4 holes

3 cut 2 slits

4 thread belt piece through slits

5 fold straight end back through belt piece and pin

6 run pointed end through buckle and pull snug around waist

pouch

1 use pouch piece and snip 6 holes

cut fringe

2 thread strap piece in and out of holes

3 gather above fringe with rubber band

4 pull straps to close pouch and tie together with a knot

Toga Time

Roman tunic

YOU'LL NEED:
- bath towel
- long T-shirt
- piece of rope

1 fold towel over shoulder

2 tie rope around waist

Grecian robe

YOU'LL NEED:
- 2 large pieces of fabric
- scissors
- ribbon

1 fold 1 piece of fabric in half

2 cut slit for neck and pull fabric over head

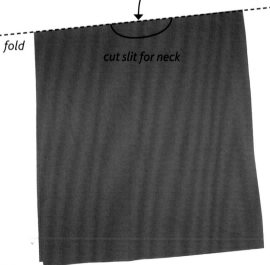

fold

cut slit for neck

3 drape second piece of fabric on head and tie ribbon around it

4 tie 1 piece of ribbon at waist

5 tie sleeves up with ribbon

6 criss-cross ribbon over chest as shown

Roman head wreath

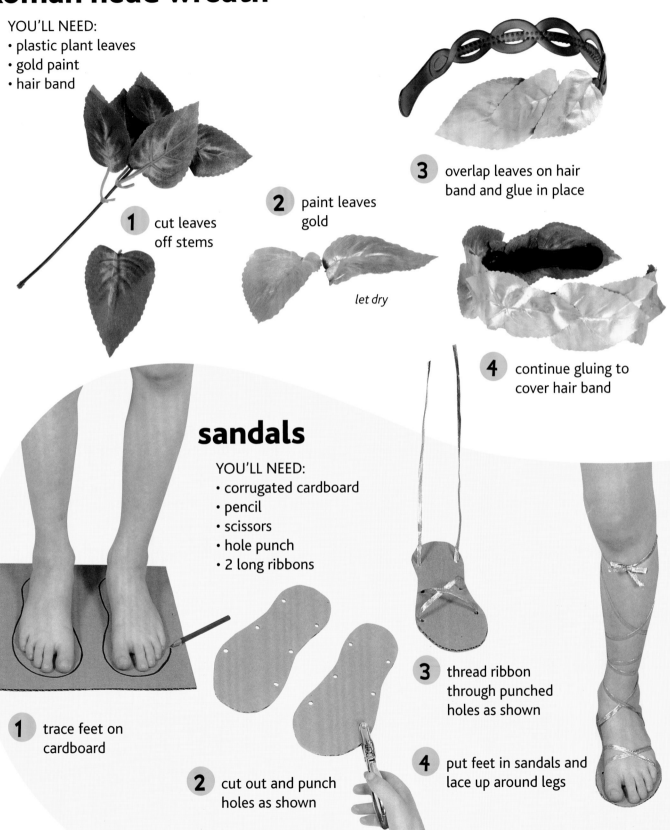

YOU'LL NEED:
- plastic plant leaves
- gold paint
- hair band

1 cut leaves off stems

2 paint leaves gold

let dry

3 overlap leaves on hair band and glue in place

4 continue gluing to cover hair band

sandals

YOU'LL NEED:
- corrugated cardboard
- pencil
- scissors
- hole punch
- 2 long ribbons

1 trace feet on cardboard

2 cut out and punch holes as shown

3 thread ribbon through punched holes as shown

4 put feet in sandals and lace up around legs

Magic Maker

YOU'LL NEED:
- large piece of fabric
- scissors
- ribbon
- pencil
- bristol board
- self-adhesive vinyl
- clear tape
- painted stir stick
- ribbons

robe

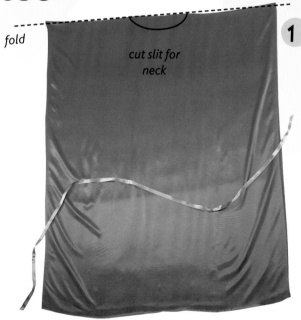

fold

cut slit for neck

1 fold fabric in half and cut slit for neck

2 pull fabric over head and tie 1 piece of ribbon around waist

3 decorate with stars

stars

1 create a star pattern by drawing a circle on bristol board and marking 5 dots as shown, then connect dots to make a star

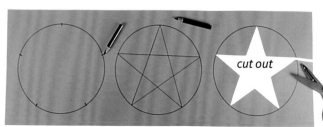

cut out

2 trace pattern onto self-adhesive vinyl

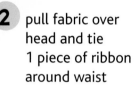

3 cut out stars and peel off backing to stick on robe

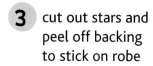

hat

1 draw shape on bristol board as shown

2 form cone so it fits head

3 fasten with tape

cut along line

4 decorate with stars

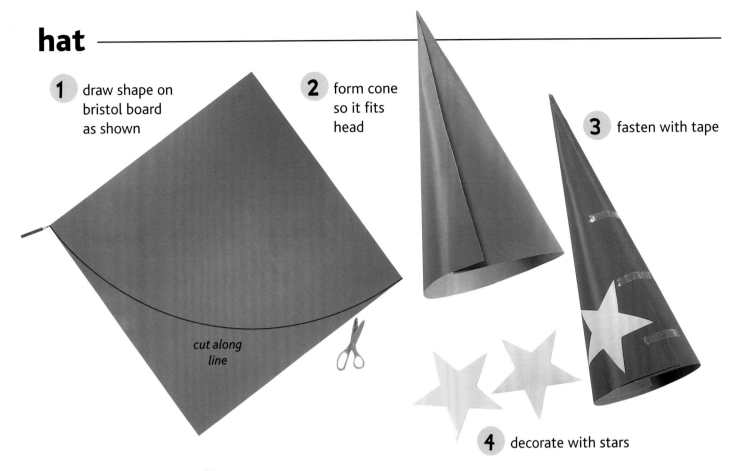

magic wand

1 fold ribbons in half

2 tape to top of painted stir stick

3 stick two vinyl stars together with top of stir stick between them

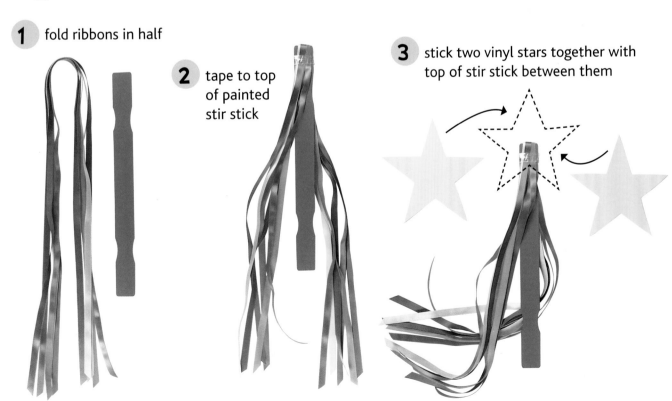

Beautiful Beading

on fishing line:

use beads with small holes

on gimp or lanyard:

fold tape at 1 end to prevent beads from falling off

on yarn:

wrap tape around 1 end for easy threading

on shoelaces:

use beads with large holes

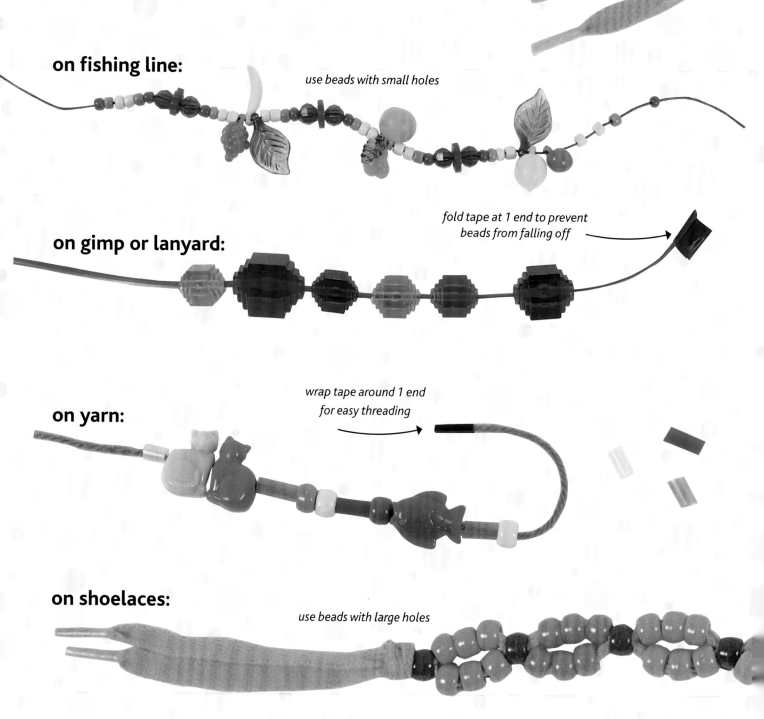

28

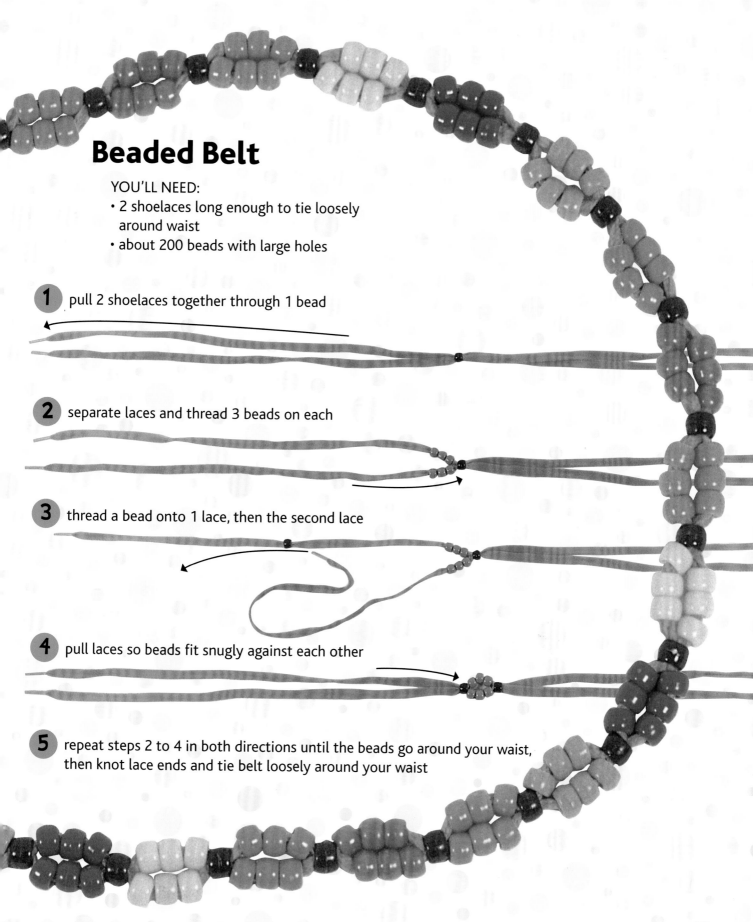

Beaded Belt

YOU'LL NEED:
- 2 shoelaces long enough to tie loosely around waist
- about 200 beads with large holes

1 pull 2 shoelaces together through 1 bead

2 separate laces and thread 3 beads on each

3 thread a bead onto 1 lace, then the second lace

4 pull laces so beads fit snugly against each other

5 repeat steps 2 to 4 in both directions until the beads go around your waist, then knot lace ends and tie belt loosely around your waist

Fit for Royalty

royal crown

Find instructions for cape on page 10.

YOU'LL NEED:
- tracing paper
- pencil
- scissors
- bristol board
- stapler
- polyester stuffing
- glue
- paper tube

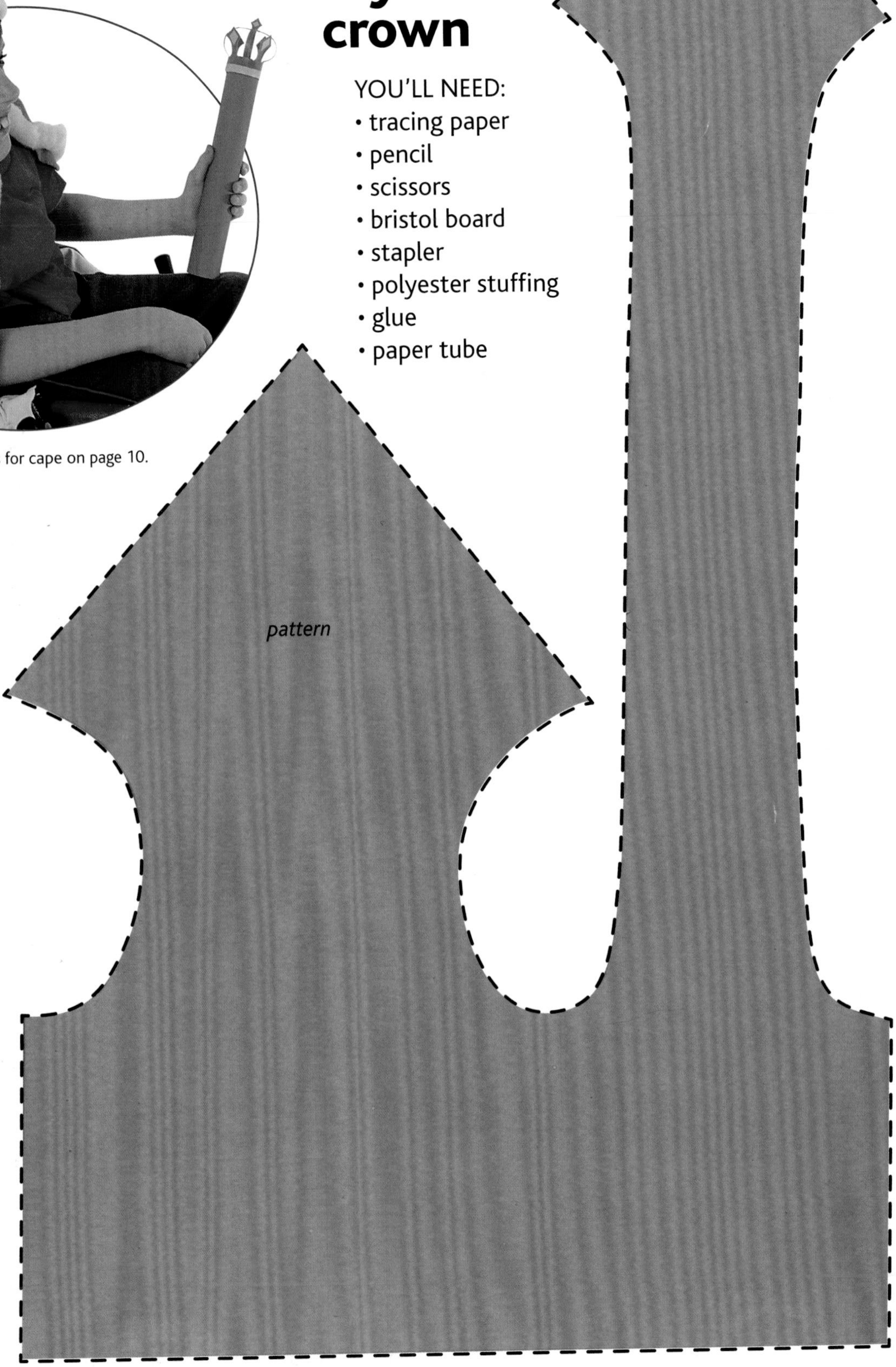

pattern

1 draw pattern onto tracing paper

cut out

2 trace outline onto bristol board 4 times as shown

cut out

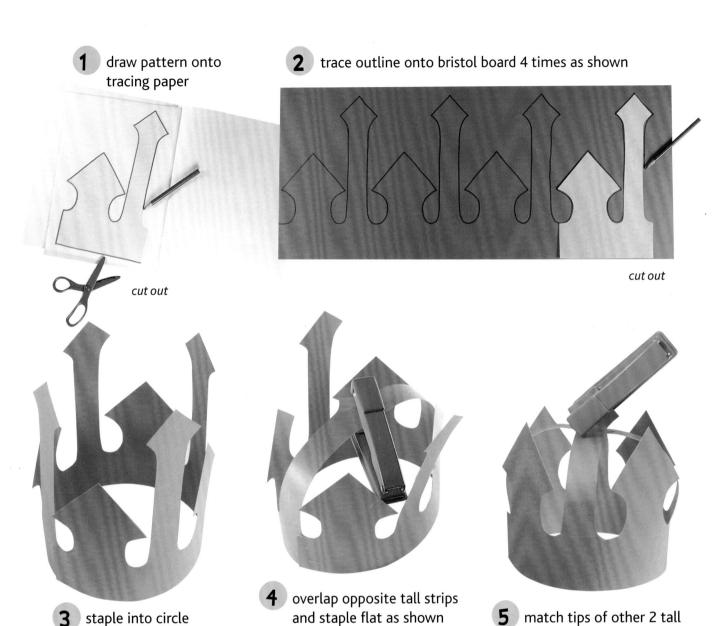

3 staple into circle to fit head

Find stapling tip on page 7.

4 overlap opposite tall strips and staple flat as shown

5 match tips of other 2 tall strips and staple upright

6 glue on stuffing and decorations

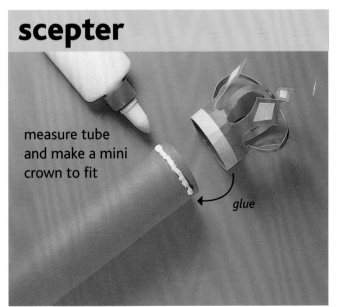

scepter

measure tube and make a mini crown to fit

glue

Orange Smile

ASK FOR ADULT HELP

YOU'LL NEED:
• orange peel
• scissors
• your smile

1 cut oval a little bigger than your smile from peel

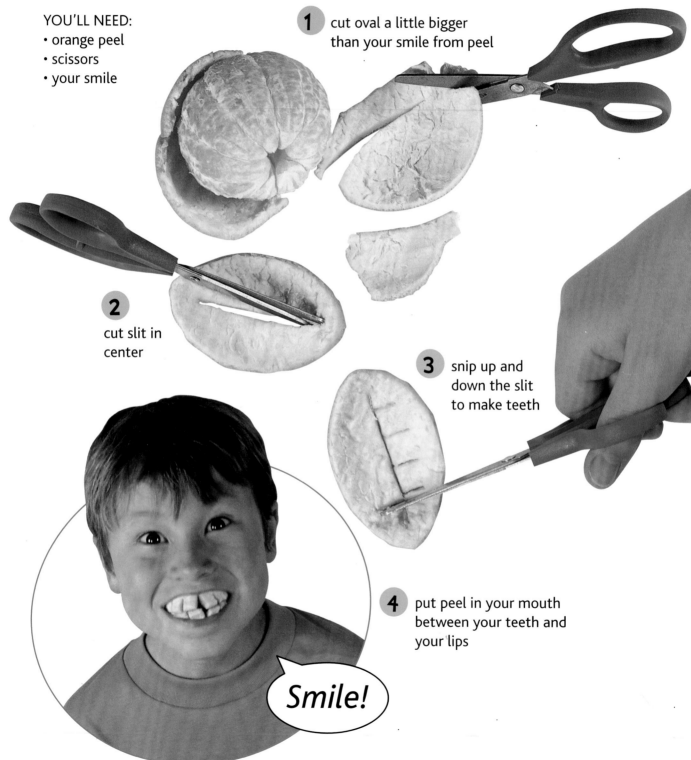

2 cut slit in center

3 snip up and down the slit to make teeth

4 put peel in your mouth between your teeth and your lips

Smile!

Ruby Ring

YOU'LL NEED:
- aluminum foil
- scissors
- white glue
- glitter

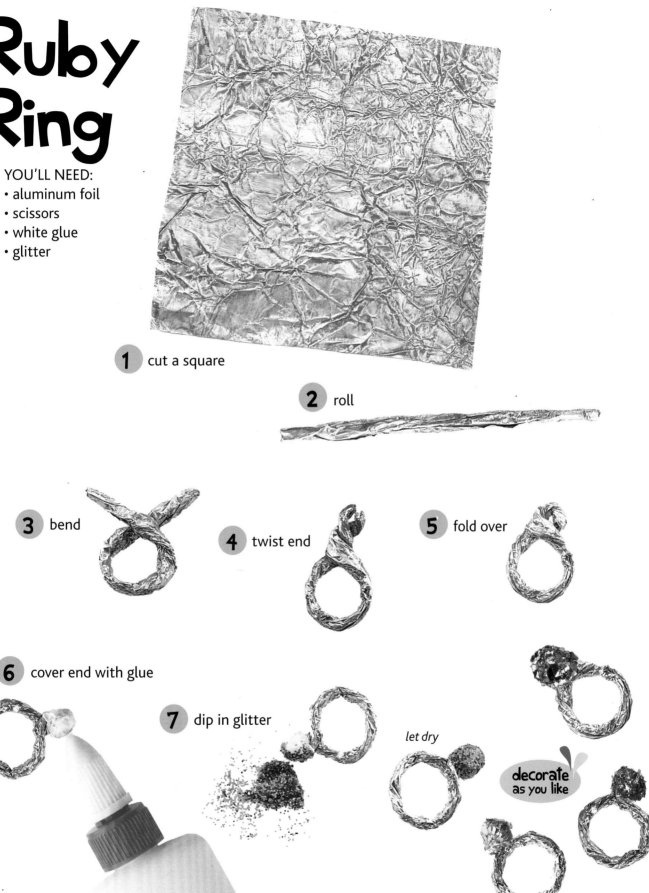

1 cut a square

2 roll

3 bend

4 twist end

5 fold over

6 cover end with glue

7 dip in glitter

let dry

decorate as you like

Rings 'n' Things

rings

YOU'LL NEED:
- buttons and beads
- yarn
- scissors

1 run yarn through bead or button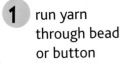

2 tie yarn to fit around finger

3 knot

4 trim ends

earrings

YOU'LL NEED:
- drinking straws
- scissors
- rings (see above or use any ring)

1 cut small pieces of straw

2 snip open as shown

3 slide straw onto ring

4 clip straw to ear

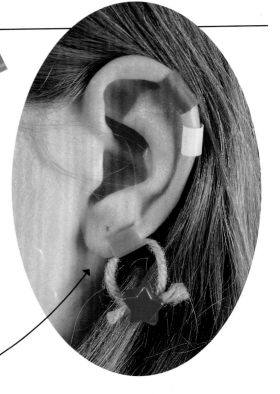

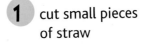

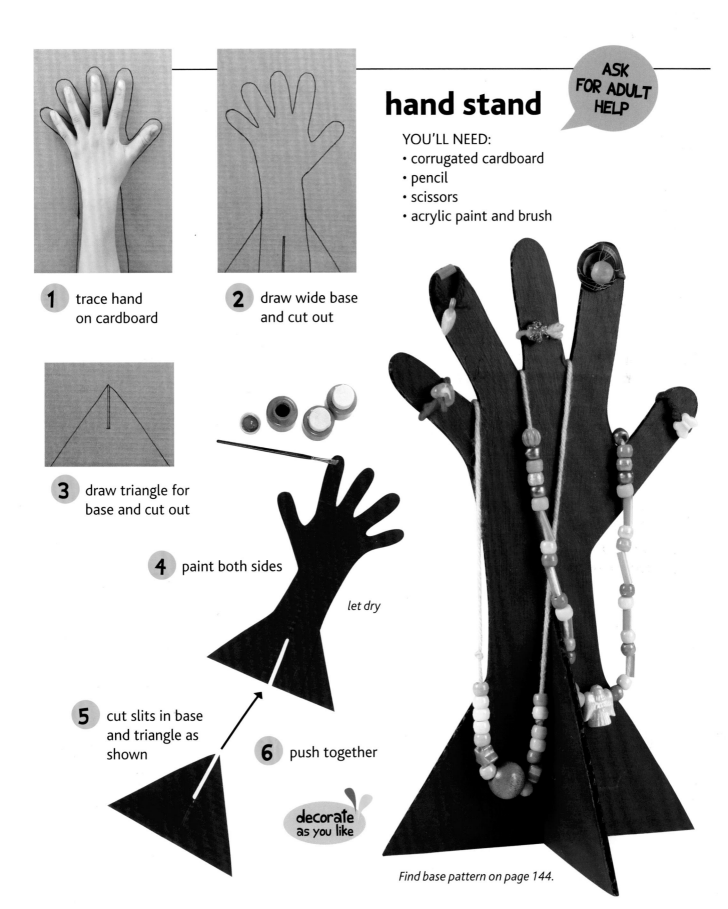

hand stand

ASK FOR ADULT HELP

YOU'LL NEED:
- corrugated cardboard
- pencil
- scissors
- acrylic paint and brush

1 trace hand on cardboard

2 draw wide base and cut out

3 draw triangle for base and cut out

4 paint both sides

let dry

5 cut slits in base and triangle as shown

6 push together

decorate as you like

Find base pattern on page 144.

35

Laced-up Locket

ASK FOR ADULT HELP

YOU'LL NEED:
- tracing paper
- pencil
- scissors
- hole punch
- bristol board
- yarn
- photo
- white glue
- large bead

1 draw pattern onto tracing paper

cut out

punch holes

pattern

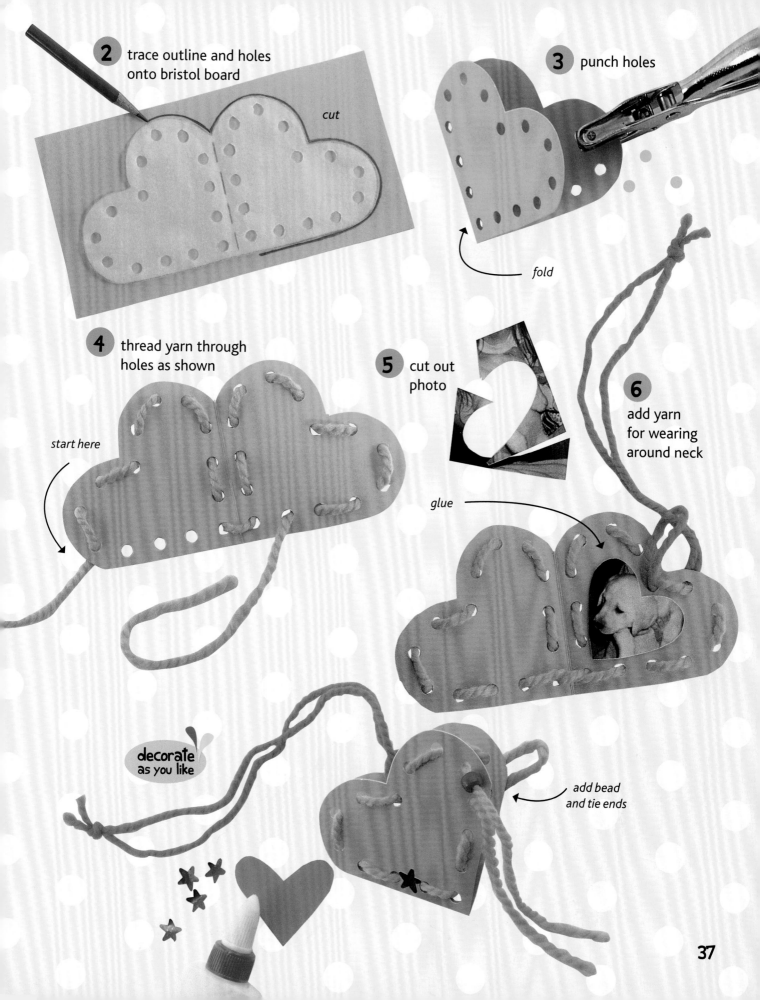

2 trace outline and holes onto bristol board

cut

3 punch holes

fold

4 thread yarn through holes as shown

start here

5 cut out photo

glue

6 add yarn for wearing around neck

decorate as you like

add bead and tie ends

37

Enchanted Castle Tower

ASK FOR ADULT HELP

YOU'LL NEED:
- 3 painted cardboard appliance boxes
- scissors
- rope
- glue
- bristol board
- tape
- colored paper
- 2 drinking straws
- tempera paint
- paintbrush

drawbridge

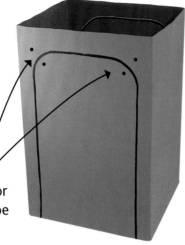

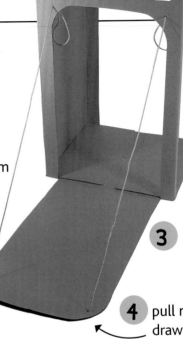

cut doors at side and back

1 poke 4 holes for drawbridge rope

2 cut out drawbridge, leaving bottom attached

3 thread rope through holes and tie

4 pull rope to close drawbridge

towers

1 cut out windows and doors as shown

2 glue boxes together with drawbridge in middle, matching open doors at side

38

flags

1 make 2 bristol board cones and tape to box tops

2 attach drinking straws and paper flags with tape and add castle details with paint

decorate as you like

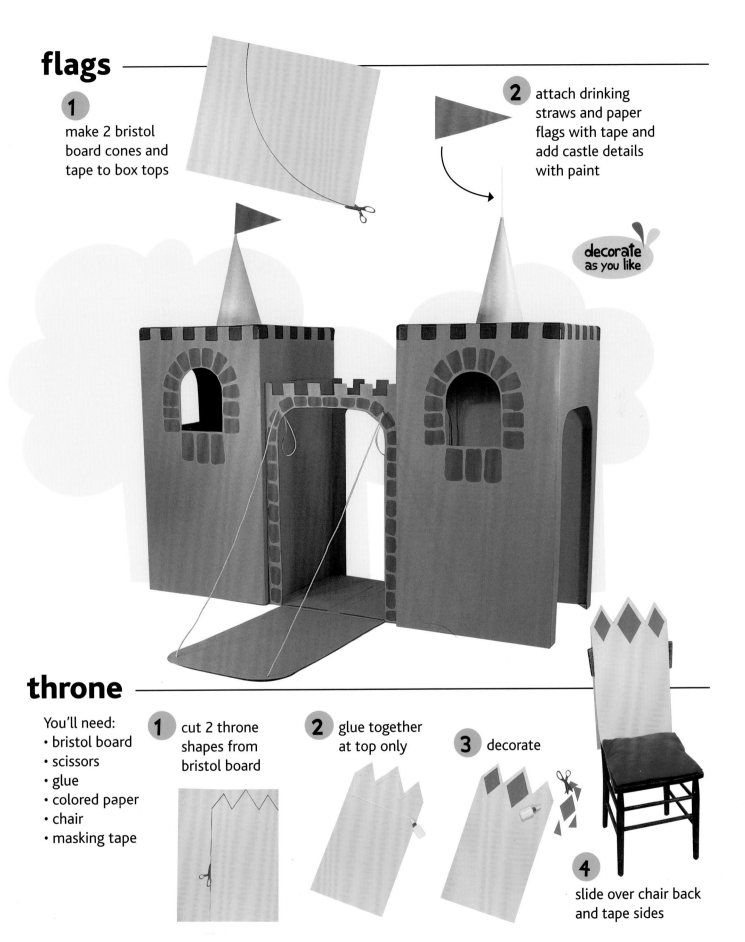

throne

You'll need:
• bristol board
• scissors
• glue
• colored paper
• chair
• masking tape

1 cut 2 throne shapes from bristol board

2 glue together at top only

3 decorate

4 slide over chair back and tape sides

Let's Make Puppets

Puppet Play

Get to know your puppet

Every puppet is special. You can give your puppets faces that show how they feel. And when you make them talk and move, they will really come alive!

1 **get your puppets to tell about themselves**
- names
- what they do every day
- favorite things, places, games
- what they like to eat and drink

I like purple pickles and pineapple punch. Let's go out for a picnic lunch.

I love to sing and dance.

Find instructions for making a puppet stage on page 62.

2 two puppets can talk to each other in different voices

- happy
- angry
- sad
- surprised
- silly
- excited
- scared

Please don't wave your wand and make my treasure disappear!

Okay. But only if you'll breathe fire so we can toast marshmallows.

3 make your puppets move

- bow
- kiss
- twist
- fall
- shake hands
- sleep
- pick things up
- put things down
- move things
- walk
- jump
- run
- chase
- dance
- push
- pull
- nod
- shake
- cry
- laugh

See us run and jump!

These are some of the ways you can play with your puppets. You can probably think of more. When you get to know your puppets, there are lots of amazing things you can say and do. Have fun!

Silly Dragon

ASK FOR ADULT HELP

YOU'LL NEED:
- bristol board
- scissors
- white glue
- old sock
- crumpled newspaper
- 2 rubber bands
- googly eyes
- needle and thread
- felt

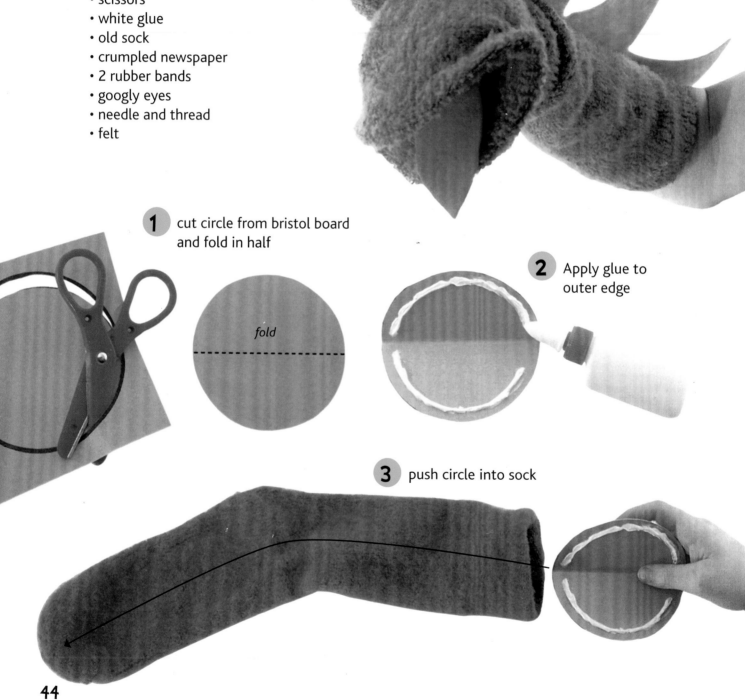

1 cut circle from bristol board and fold in half

fold

2 Apply glue to outer edge

3 push circle into sock

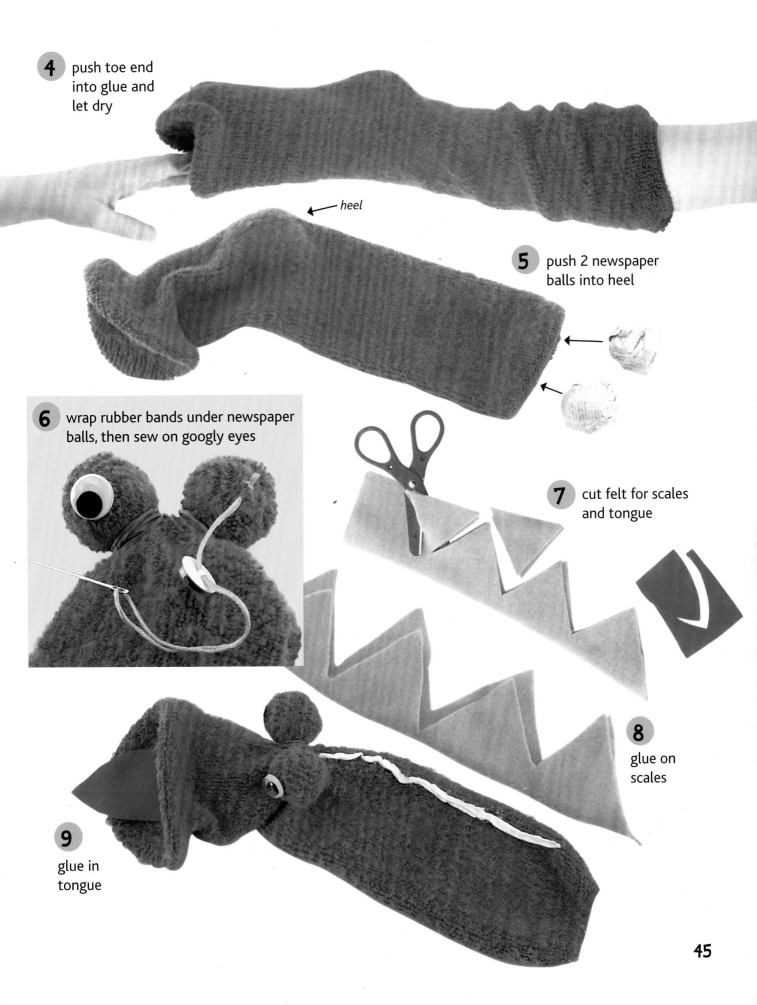

4 push toe end into glue and let dry

heel

5 push 2 newspaper balls into heel

6 wrap rubber bands under newspaper balls, then sew on googly eyes

7 cut felt for scales and tongue

8 glue on scales

9 glue in tongue

45

Wonderful Wizard

ASK FOR ADULT HELP

YOU'LL NEED:
- small paper tube
- scissors
- paper towel
- white glue
- water
- soupspoon
- plastic container
- markers or colored tape
- bristol board
- clear tape
- facecloth
- star stickers

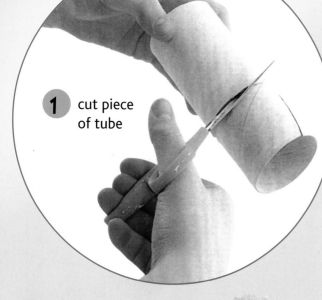

1 cut piece of tube

2 tear paper towel into pieces

3 mix together 3 soupspoons of glue and 3 soupspoons of water

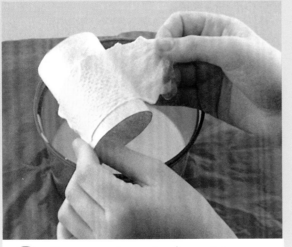

4 dip paper pieces in glue mixture and cover outside of tube

5 shape dipped paper pieces for nose and ears, and let dry

6 add details with markers or pieces of colored tape

7 cut bristol board shape for hat as shown

8 form into cone and tape

9 glue onto head

10 cover hand with facecloth, then tape around little finger and thumb to form arms

decorate with stars

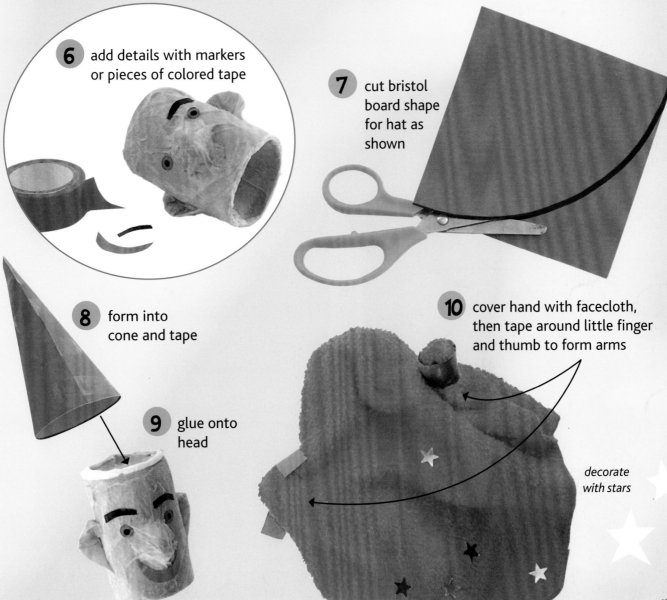

String King

YOU'LL NEED:
- felt
- scissors
- bristol board
- markers
- painted toilet paper tube
- hole punch
- 6 paper fasteners
- string
- paper towel tube

1 cut cape, arms, and legs from felt

2 cut head from bristol board

3 draw details with markers

4 punch 6 holes in toilet paper tube

5 punch holes in felt

6 push paper fasteners from inside of tube to attach arms and legs

7 attach head and cape

8 loop and tie strings around paper towel tube

9 tie string to end of arms and top of crown

decorate as you like

Ta-daaa!

Turn the page to make a horse for your king to ride.

Prancing Pony

YOU'LL NEED:
- tracing paper
- pencil
- scissors
- bristol board
- hole punch
- 6 paper fasteners
- yarn
- colored paper
- glue
- paint stir stick

1 draw pattern pieces onto tracing paper

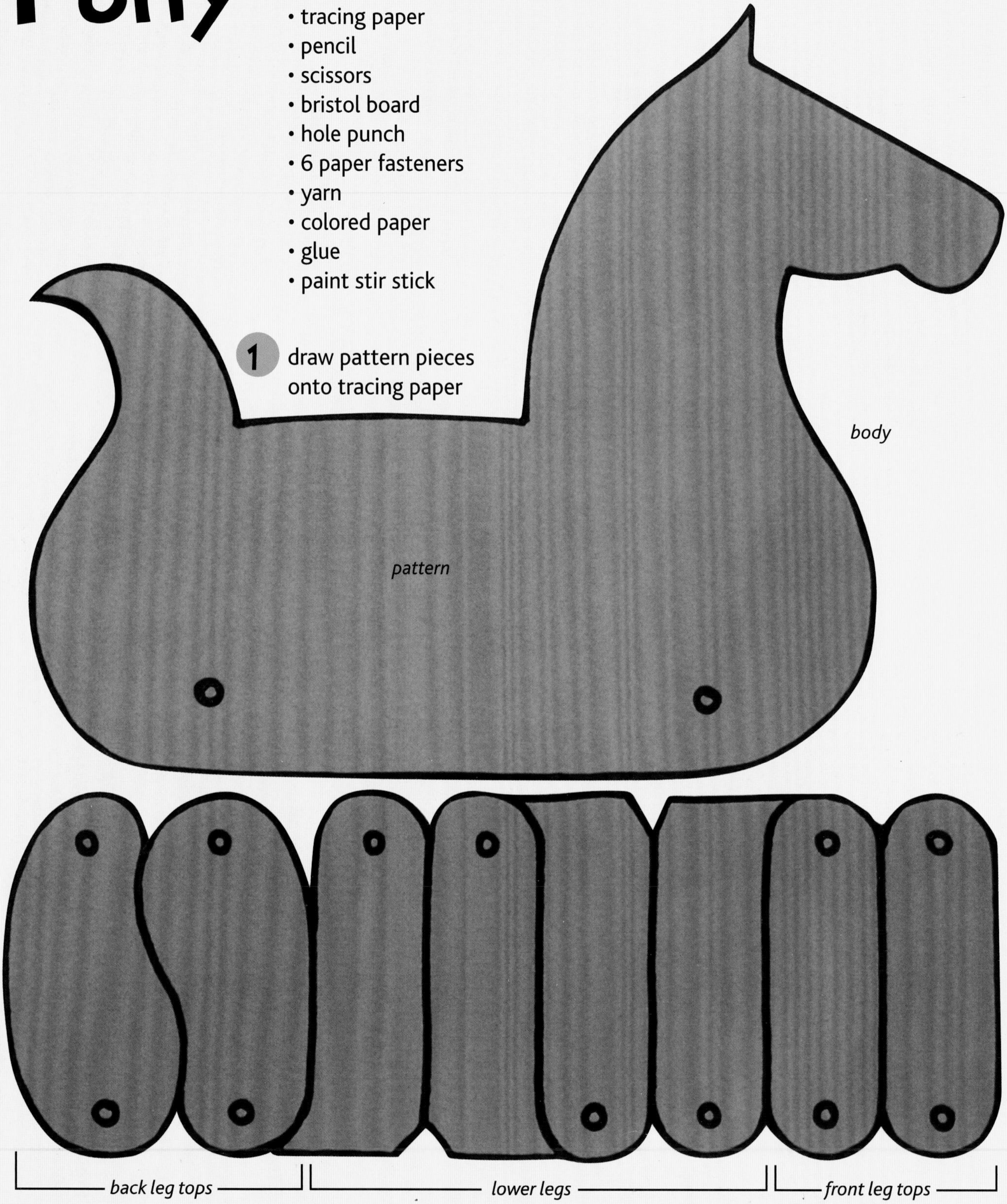

body

pattern

back leg tops

lower legs

front leg tops

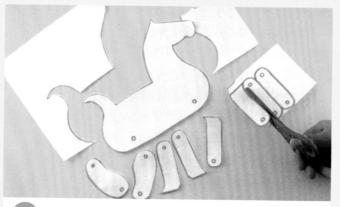

2 cut out pieces

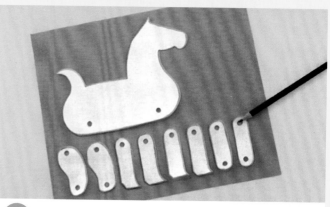

3 trace shapes and holes onto bristol board

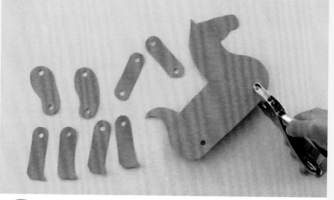

4 cut out shapes and punch holes

5 attach leg tops to body with 2 fasteners

6 attach lower legs with 4 fasteners

7 cut and glue paper and yarn details

8 glue stir stick on back and let dry

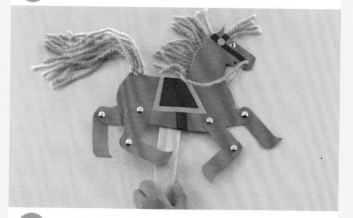

9 jiggle stick to make pony prance

Rosie Rock Star

ASK FOR ADULT HELP

YOU'LL NEED:
- paint stir stick
- toilet paper tube
- stocking
- scissors
- 2 rubber bands
- felt
- stapler
- yarn
- glue
- markers

1 slide tube onto stick

2 cut foot off stocking

3 pull stocking over tube

4 secure ends to stick with rubber bands

5 slide tube down over 1 rubber band

6 cut hands from felt and staple onto stocking

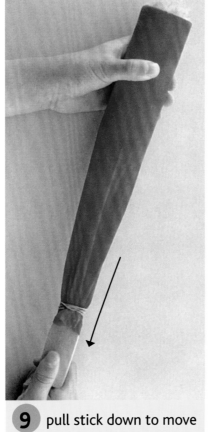

7 glue yarn on back of stick for hair

let dry

draw face with markers

fluff hair

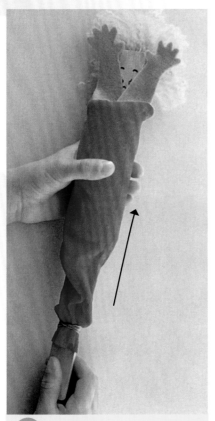

8 hold tube and bottom of stick

9 pull stick down to move puppet into tube

10 push stick up to make Rosie pop out

Handy Miniatures

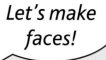
Let's make faces!

YOU'LL NEED:
- your own hands
- washable markers
- yarn
- bottle tops
- tissue paper
- scarf

happy hair

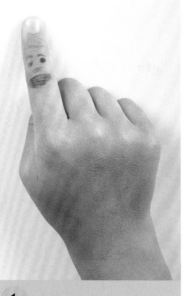

1 draw face

2 put yarn on finger

3 place bottle top over yarn

thumb chum

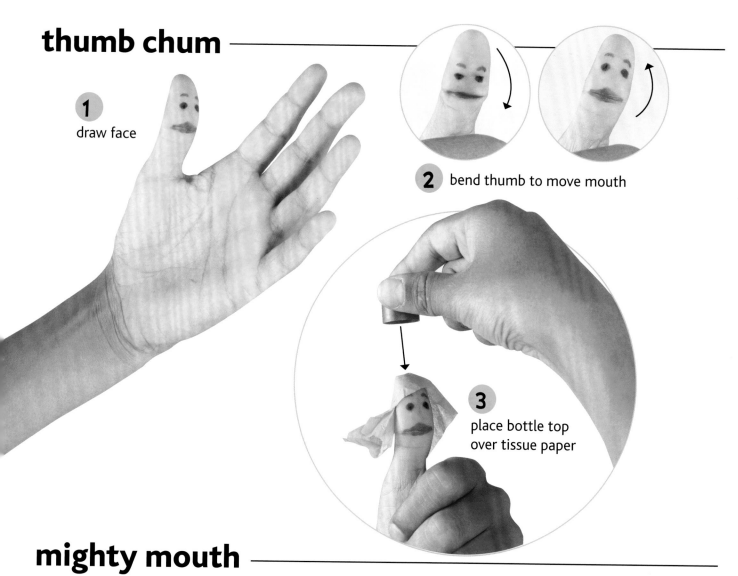

1 draw face

2 bend thumb to move mouth

3 place bottle top over tissue paper

mighty mouth

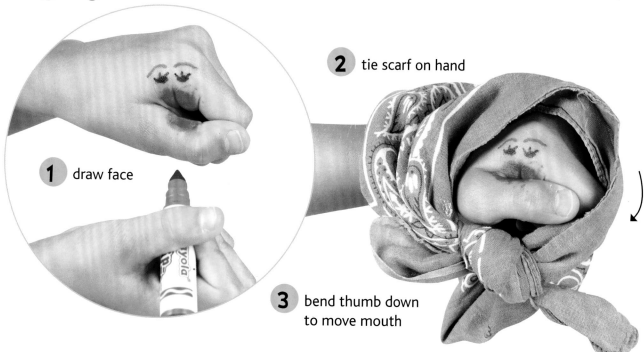

1 draw face

2 tie scarf on hand

3 bend thumb down to move mouth

Finger Wigglers

decorate as you like

YOU'LL NEED:
- bristol board
- pencil
- scissors
- clear tape
- button
- markers

gabby gator

1 fold bristol board and draw mouth

2 add nostrils and teeth

3 cut out shape

snip off bottom nostrils

4 cut strips for finger rings

include eye bumps on 1

5 tape strips into rings

6 tape rings to outside of head

fold eyes up

fold nostrils up

fold teeth down

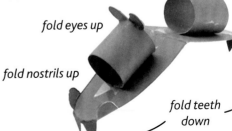

tweeter

1 cut out bird and beak

fold beak and glue on

2 cut strips for finger rings

3 tape rings to back of wings

move fingers in and out to flap wings

elephant

1 draw outline on bristol board

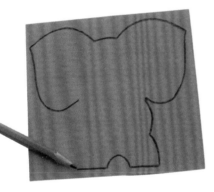

2 trace button for 3 holes and cut out

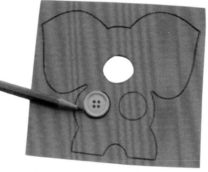

have a grown-up help you start cutting the holes

3 cut out and draw details with markers

sunshine

1 cut body from bristol board

2 fold up feet, then draw details with markers

3 cut strips and tape into finger rings

4 tape rings to back of legs

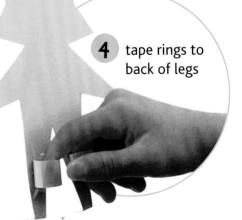

Finger Friends

YOU'LL NEED:
- colored construction paper
- scissors
- markers
- clear tape
- white glue

decorate as you like

queen

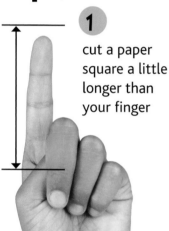

1 cut a paper square a little longer than your finger

2 cut points for crown

3 draw details with markers

4 tape into tube

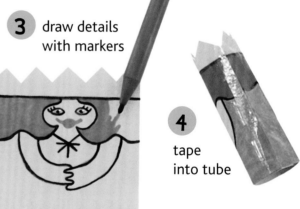

rabbit

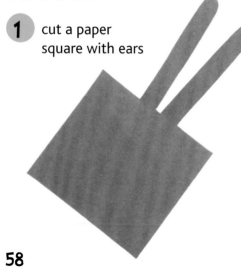

1 cut a paper square with ears

2 draw details with markers, then glue on paper whiskers

3 tape into tube

mouse

1 cut a paper square a little longer than your finger

2 cut shape for head

draw details with markers

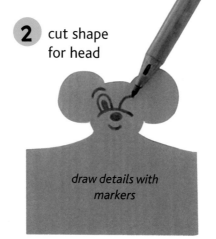

3 tape into tube and add paper tail

miss muffet

2 cut halfway down to make hair

1 cut a paper rectangle about twice as long as your finger

draw details with markers

3 tape into tube

spider

1 cut a paper rectangle a little longer than your finger

2 cut 8 legs, leaving a strip on top

3 tape into ring

4 glue on paper eyes

bend legs

59

Pink Pig

YOU'LL NEED:
- 2 soft sponges
- marker
- scissors
- white glue
- googly eyes
- fabric paint

decorate as you like

1 draw 3 lines on sponge as shown

2 cut short lines partway through

3 cut long line all the way through

4 try on and adjust cuts as needed

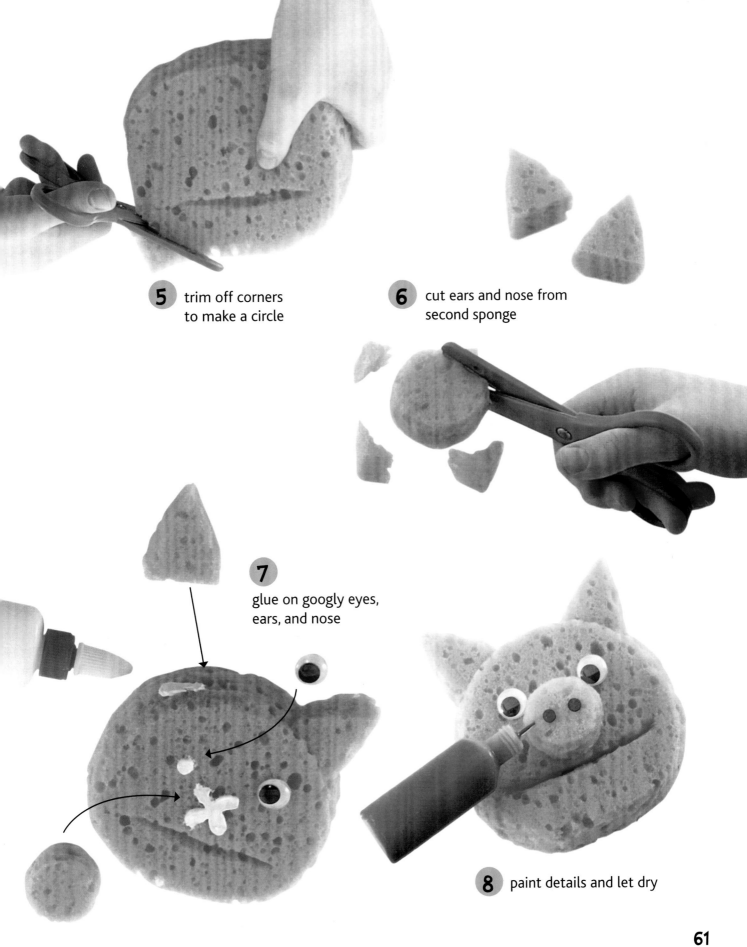

5 trim off corners to make a circle

6 cut ears and nose from second sponge

7 glue on googly eyes, ears, and nose

8 paint details and let dry

Puppet Stage

ASK FOR ADULT HELP

YOU'LL NEED:
- 2 chairs
- 4 large towels
- broomstick
- 2 large safety pins
- construction paper
- tape
- markers

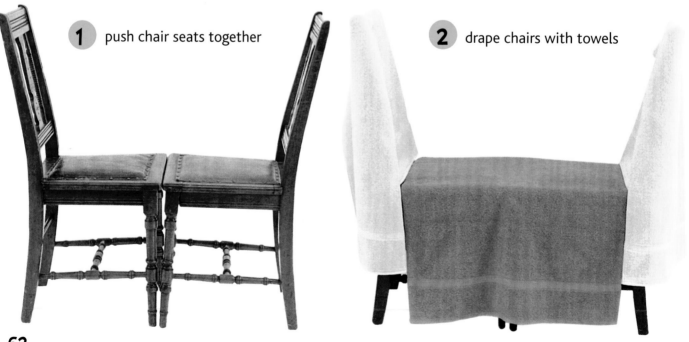

1 push chair seats together

2 drape chairs with towels

3 balance broomstick on chair backs

drape towel over broomstick and secure with safety pins

4 cut out construction paper decorations

decorate as you like

5 tape decorations to towels and broom

Putting on a Puppet Play

- Make puppets talk to each other or to the audience.
- Have only 1 puppet speak at a time.
- Move only the puppet that is speaking.
- Hold the puppet so the audience can see its face.
- Act out a fairy tale or tell a story.

Kid-Sized Collage

YOU'LL NEED:
- large piece of paper
- pencil
- scissors
- crayons, markers, paint, and brush
- white glue
- buttons
- colored paper
- fabric and yarn
- masking tape
- a friend to help

1 trace around your friend's body

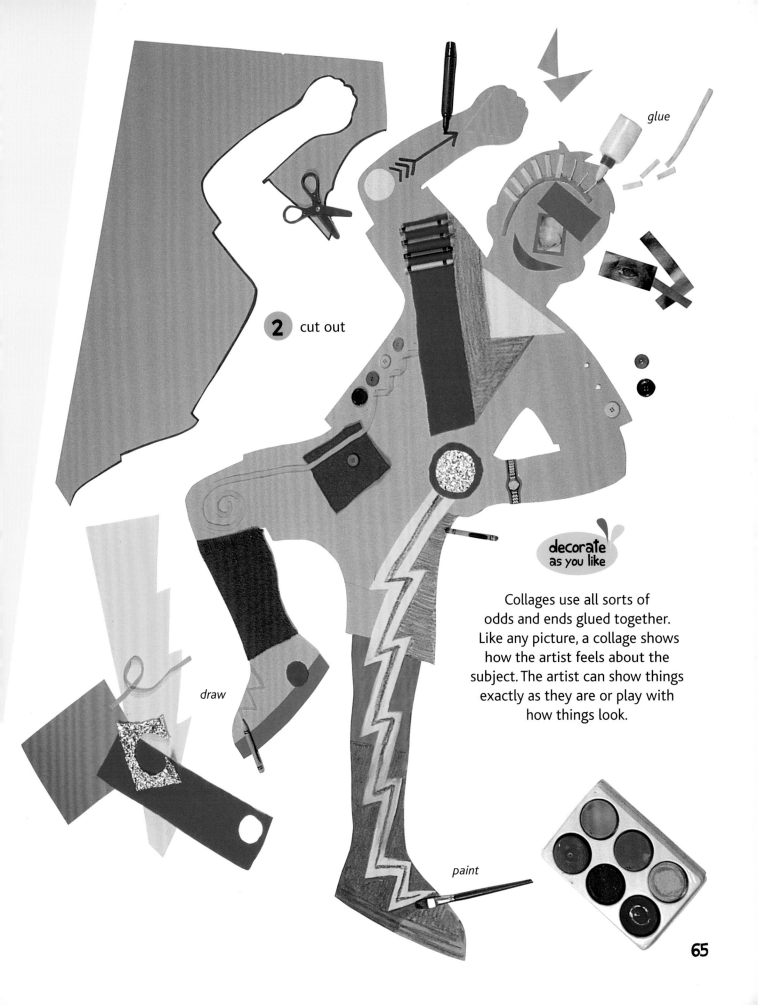

2 cut out

glue

draw

paint

decorate
as you like

Collages use all sorts of
odds and ends glued together.
Like any picture, a collage shows
how the artist feels about the
subject. The artist can show things
exactly as they are or play with
how things look.

Let's Make Nature Crafts

Respecting Nature

- Before collecting grass, moss, leaves, flowers, or twigs, ask a grown-up to make sure they are not harmful.
- Don't eat wild berries unless a grown-up tells you they are not poisonous.
- Pick only small amounts of growing things, and only what you need.
- Don't pull a plant up by its roots.
- Never take all the leaves, flowers, or seeds from a plant.
- If there are only a few plants of one kind growing, leave them alone.
- Sometimes it's better just to look, not pick, and take the memory home.

Grassy Head

YOU'LL NEED:
- end of a stocking
- potting soil
- twist ties
- rubber bands
- googly eyes
- white glue
- spoonful of grass seed
- shallow bowl
- water
- scissors

Let's get growing!

1 put several handfuls of soil in stocking

2 shape soil into round head and close with twist tie

back of head

3 pinch soil at front to make nose and wrap with rubber band

4 pinch soil at sides to make ears and wrap with rubber bands

5 glue on googly eyes and let dry

6 undo twist tie and open stocking

7 place grass seed on soil at top of head

8 close stocking and refasten with twist tie

9 shape glasses from twist ties

10 soak head in water for a few minutes, then place in shallow bowl and keep in sunny spot, making sure to add water every day

In about 10 days the grass will sprout. You can trim the grass hair or leave it long.

Cornhusk Dolls

YOU'LL NEED:
- cornhusks and silk from a raw ear of corn
- scissors
- yarn
- acrylic paint
- paintbrush

green girl and boy

1 pull husks off ears of corn, saving corn silk

2 trim thick bottoms off husks

3 layer 3 husks and place corn silk across middle

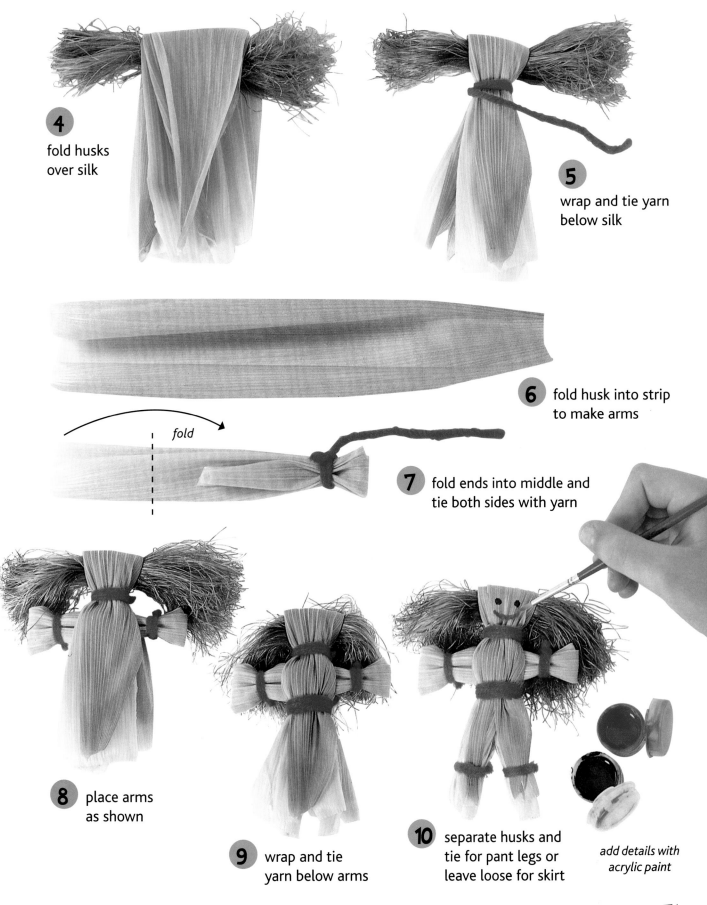

4 fold husks over silk

5 wrap and tie yarn below silk

6 fold husk into strip to make arms

fold

7 fold ends into middle and tie both sides with yarn

8 place arms as shown

9 wrap and tie yarn below arms

10 separate husks and tie for pant legs or leave loose for skirt

add details with acrylic paint

dried duo

YOU'LL NEED:
- cornhusk dolls
- tempera paint
- water
- paintbrush
- fabric
- scissors
- yarn

1 cornhusks will dry from green to golden in about a week

2 add details with tempera paint and water, and let dry

72

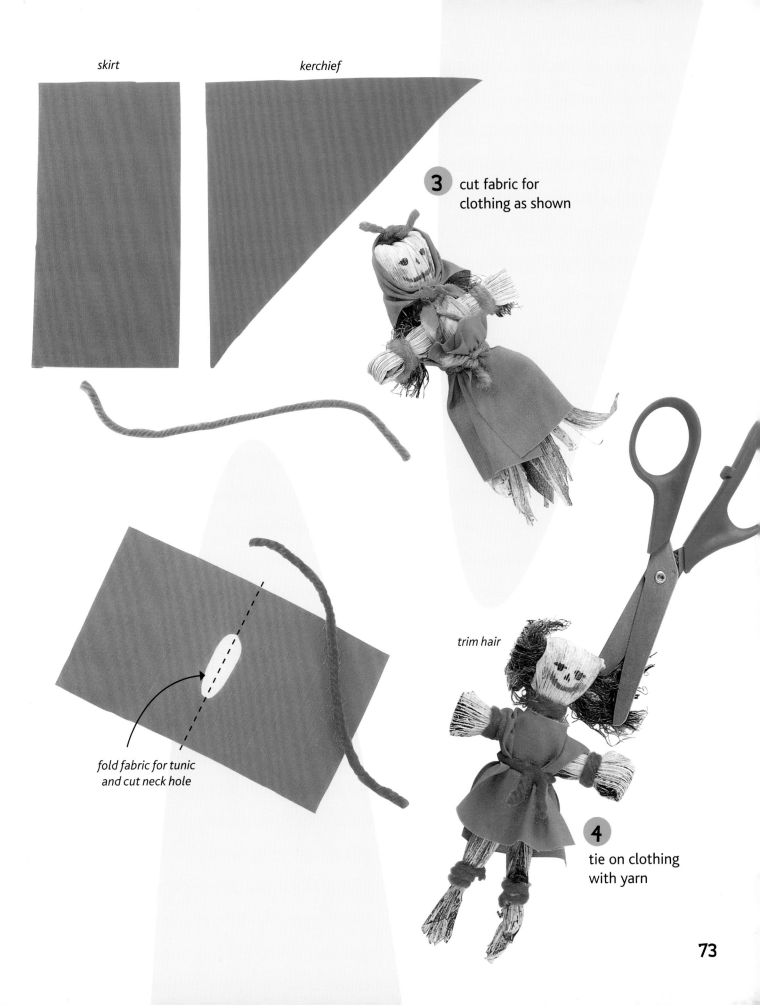

skirt

kerchief

3 cut fabric for clothing as shown

fold fabric for tunic and cut neck hole

trim hair

4 tie on clothing with yarn

73

Forest Folk

YOU'LL NEED:
- twigs
- leaves and grass
- yarn
- acrylic paint
- paintbrush
- modeling clay
- pine needles
- scissors

decorate as you like

twiggy

1 fold grass in half

2 wrap and tie grass onto twig with yarn

3 wrap and tie on leaves

4 add details in acrylic paint

5 push twig into ball of modeling clay to stand

maple man

1 cross twigs as shown

2 wrap and tie on leaf with yarn

3 tie yarn around twigs to hold them

hula

1 trim grass evenly to create skirt

2 wrap and tie pine needles to head with yarn

3 wrap and tie grass skirt to twig

twig tent

1 bundle twigs and tie with yarn at one end

2 tuck leaf stem into yarn

3 spread twigs at bottom

Twig Vase

YOU'LL NEED:
- empty jar or can
- twigs
- 2 rubber bands
- yarn

I'm sticking around!

1 break twigs so they're about the same length as can

2 put rubber bands around can

3

pull out rubber bands and insert twig as shown

4

repeat until twigs cover outside of can

5

wrap and tie yarn to cover rubber bands

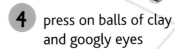

spider

YOU'LL NEED:
- 4 twist ties
- half walnut shell
- modeling clay
- googly eyes

1 line up twist ties and twist together in the middle

2 place twist ties in painted walnut shell

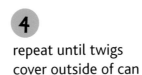

3 secure with a ball of clay

4 press on balls of clay and googly eyes

5 attach spider to vase with clay

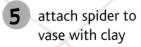

A Growing Gift

ASK FOR ADULT HELP

YOU'LL NEED:
- plant pot with saucer
- acrylic paint
- paintbrush
- wire hanger
- ribbon
- masking tape
- potting soil
- nasturtium seeds
- paper tag

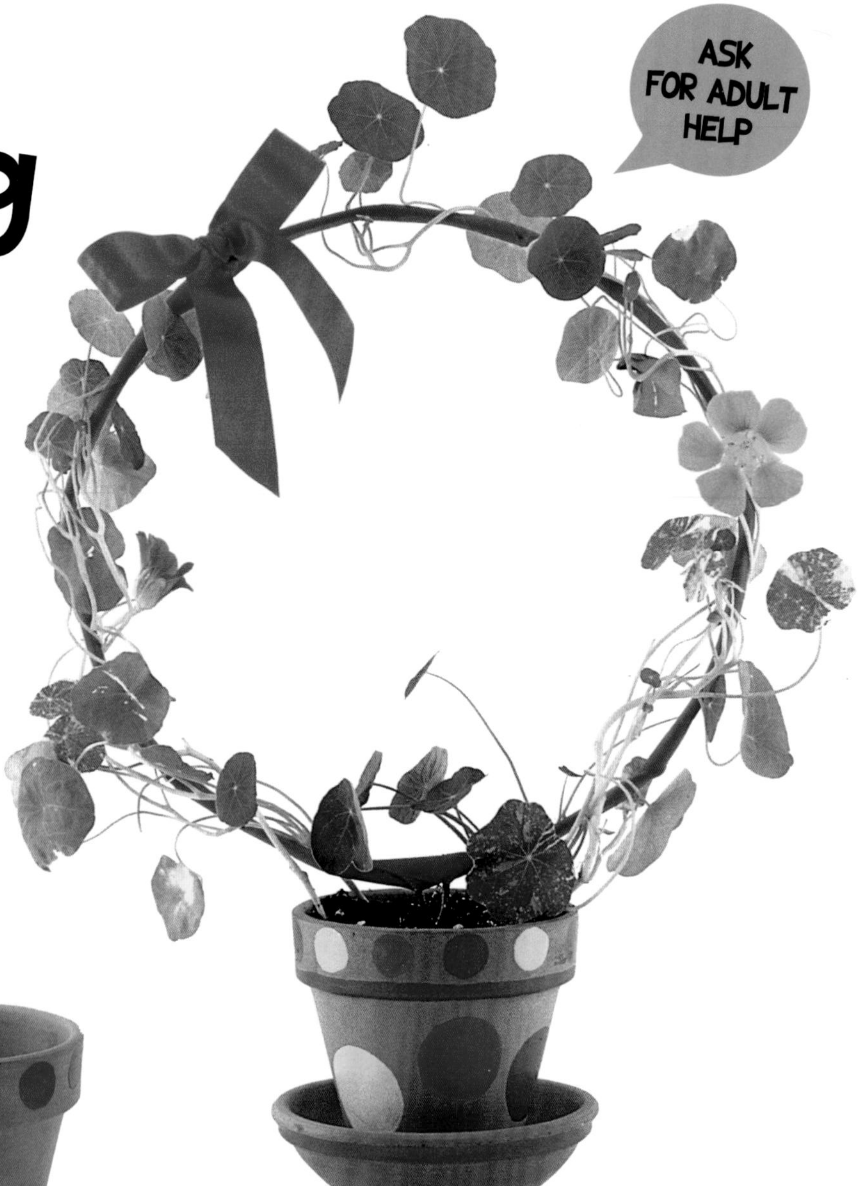

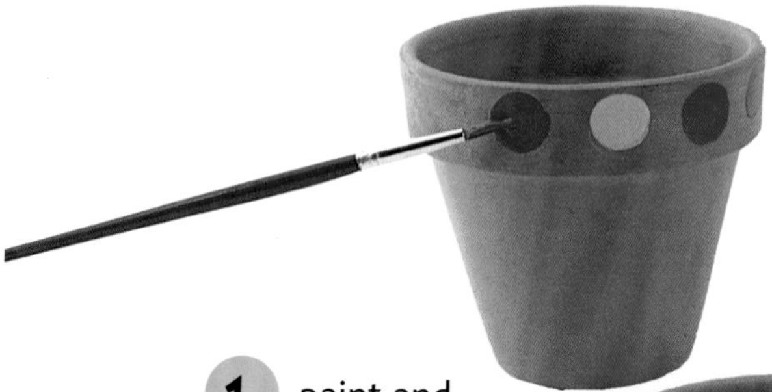

1 paint and let dry

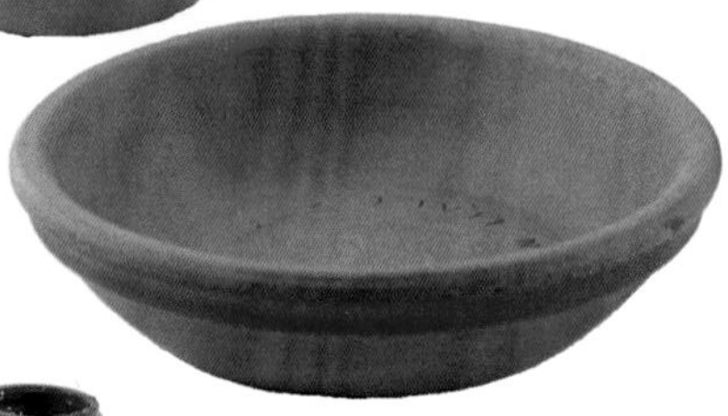

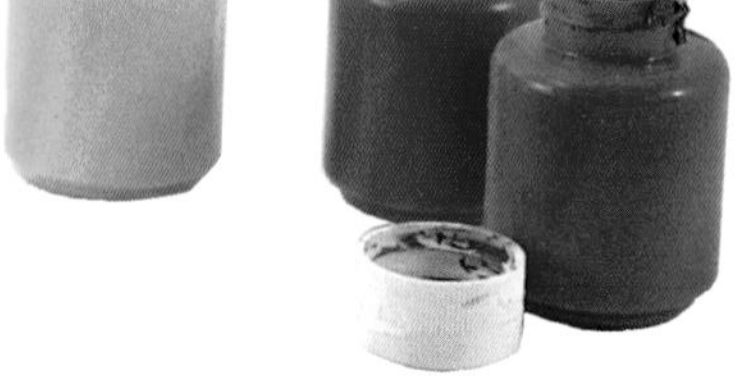

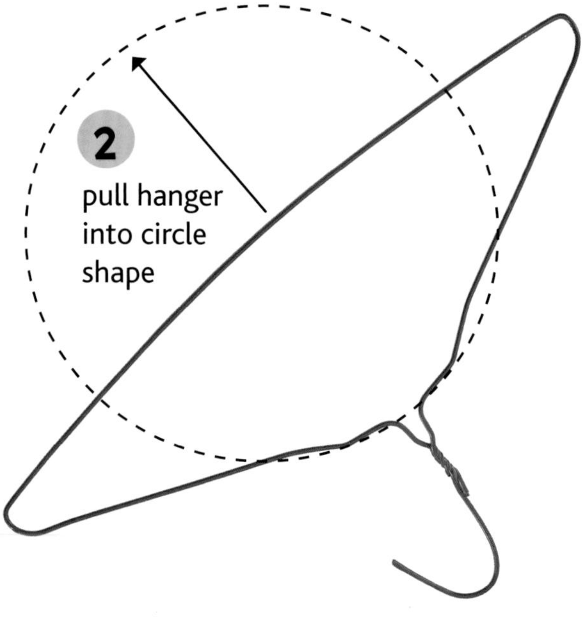

2 pull hanger into circle shape

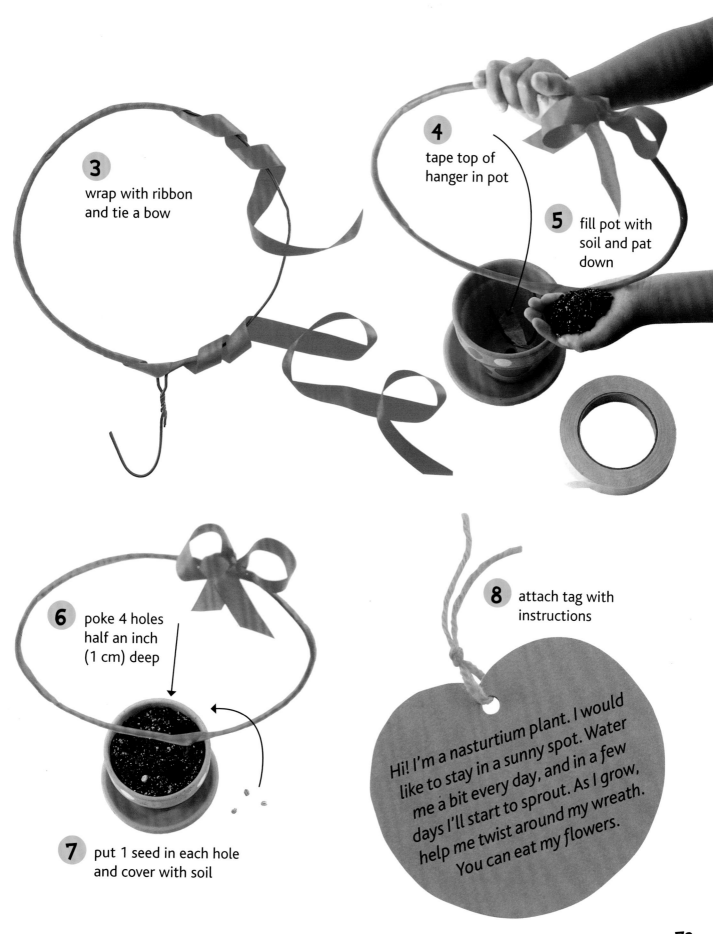

3 wrap with ribbon and tie a bow

4 tape top of hanger in pot

5 fill pot with soil and pat down

6 poke 4 holes half an inch (1 cm) deep

7 put 1 seed in each hole and cover with soil

8 attach tag with instructions

Hi! I'm a nasturtium plant. I would like to stay in a sunny spot. Water me a bit every day, and in a few days I'll start to sprout. As I grow, help me twist around my wreath. You can eat my flowers.

Moss Garden

YOU'LL NEED:
- several spoonfuls of moss
- shallow plant pot
- potting soil
- twigs
- stones
- shells
- water

decorate as you like

1 collect moss from damp places among trees or along roadsides

2 fill shallow plant pot with potting soil

3 shape soil into valleys and hills

4 make holes and dents in soil

5 press in moss

6 push in twigs

7 add stones and shells to cover all soil

8 water lightly twice a week and keep away from direct sunlight

Treasure Trunk

YOU'LL NEED:
- egg carton
- acrylic paint
- paintbrush
- 3 spoonfuls fine sand
- 3 small containers
- cardboard
- scissors
- food coloring
- white glue

1 paint egg carton with acrylic paint and let dry

2 put 1 spoonful of sand in each container

3 cut cardboard to fit top of carton

4 mix food coloring into sand

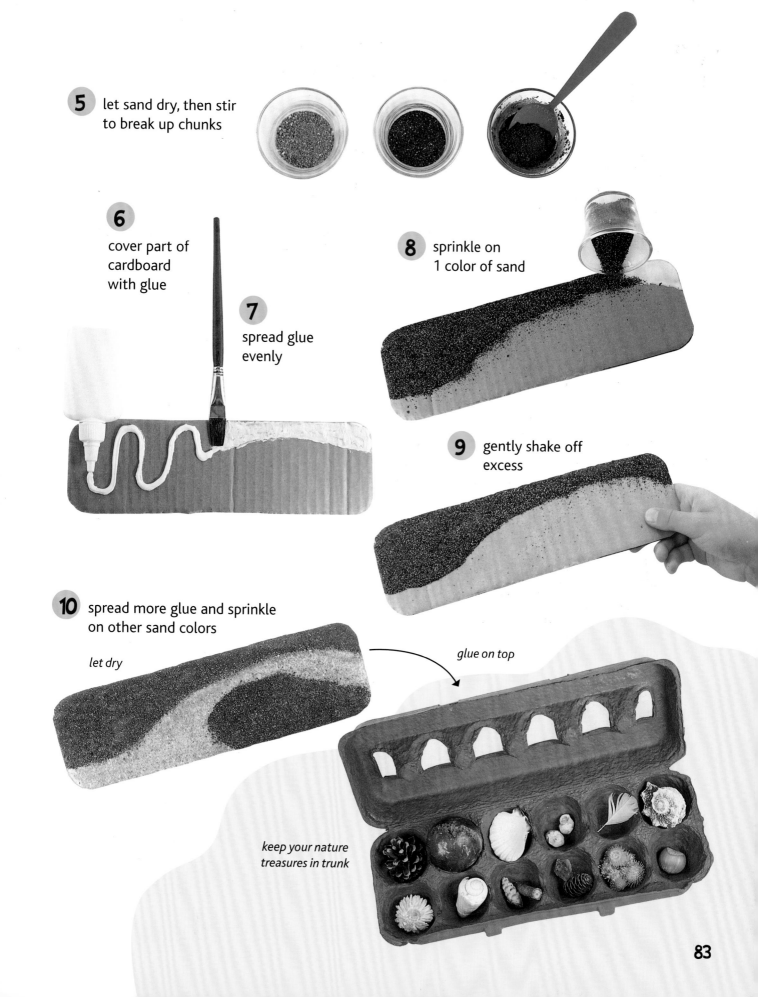

5 let sand dry, then stir to break up chunks

6 cover part of cardboard with glue

7 spread glue evenly

8 sprinkle on 1 color of sand

9 gently shake off excess

10 spread more glue and sprinkle on other sand colors

let dry

glue on top

keep your nature treasures in trunk

Precious Pets

store your pets in the pouch

pets

YOU'LL NEED:
- small smooth stones
- paper
- pencil crayons
- acrylic paint and brush

1 wash and dry stones to go in pouch

2 plan animal designs on paper

3 choose a design and draw it on a stone

4 paint over design and add details if you like

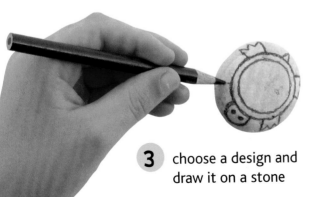

pouch

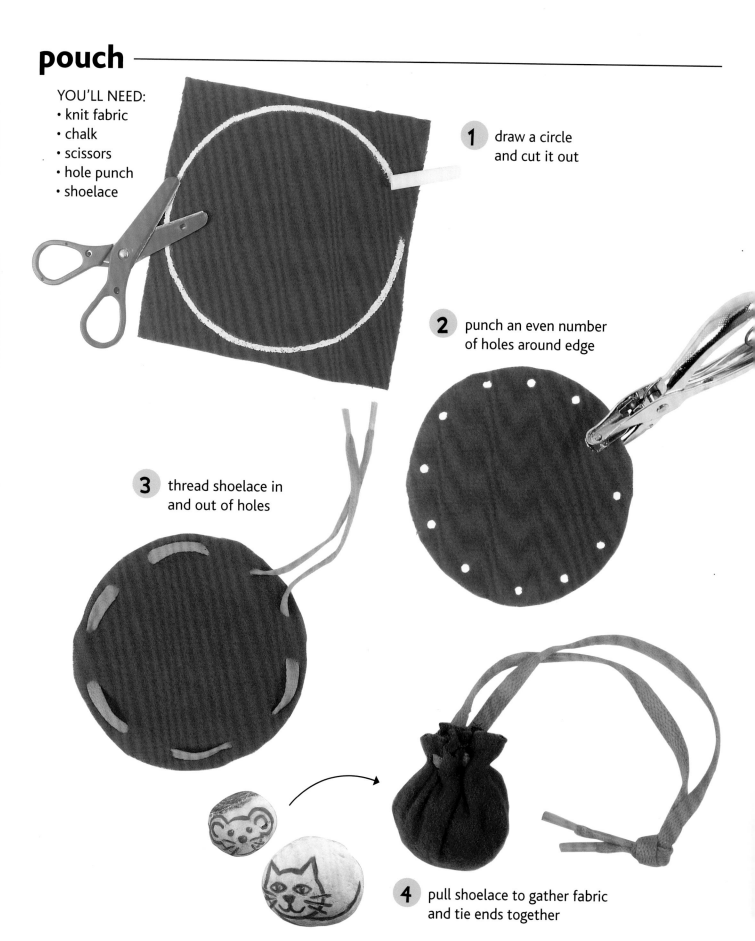

YOU'LL NEED:
• knit fabric
• chalk
• scissors
• hole punch
• shoelace

1 draw a circle and cut it out

2 punch an even number of holes around edge

3 thread shoelace in and out of holes

4 pull shoelace to gather fabric and tie ends together

Let's Make Toys

Toy Train

decorate as you like

YOU'LL NEED:
- corrugated cardboard
- scissors
- round toothpicks
- foam trays
- pencil
- large button
- white glue
- modeling clay
- paper tube
- small boxes
- colored paper clips

1 cut platforms out of painted cardboard

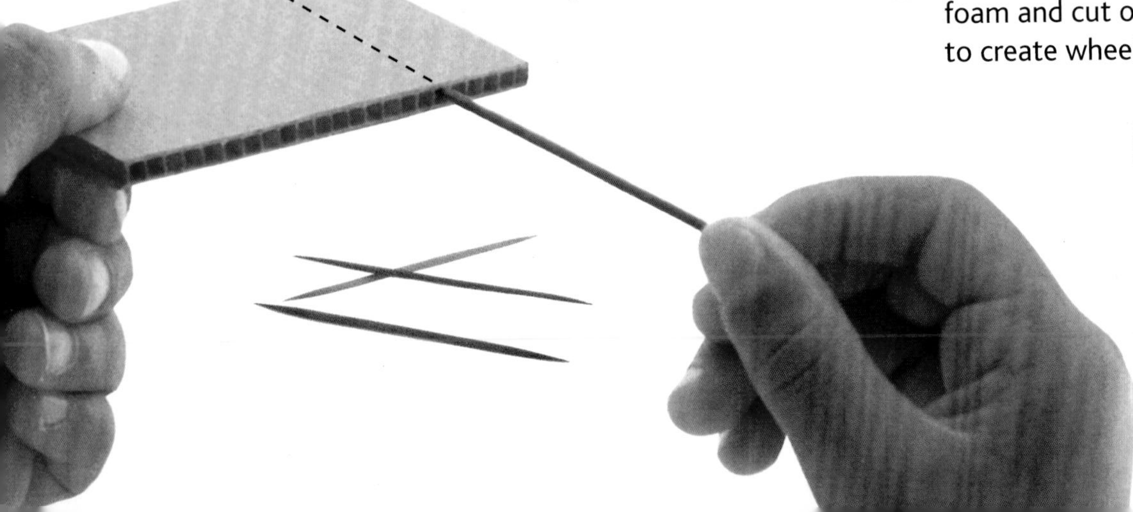

2 push 2 toothpicks through slats

3 trace button on foam and cut out to create wheels

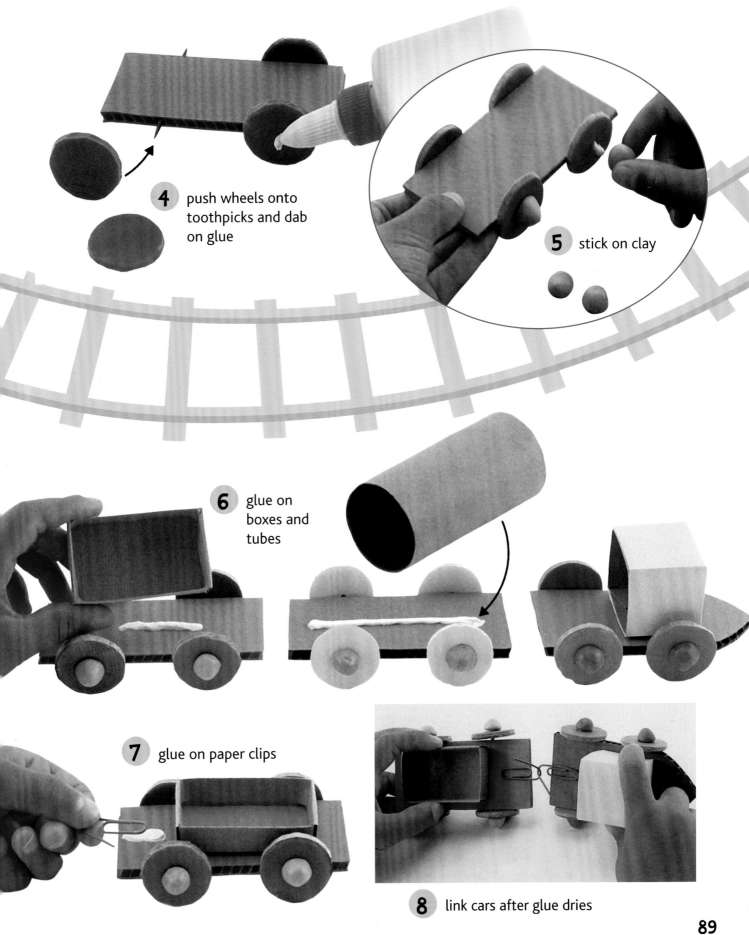

4 push wheels onto toothpicks and dab on glue

5 stick on clay

6 glue on boxes and tubes

7 glue on paper clips

8 link cars after glue dries

89

Race Car

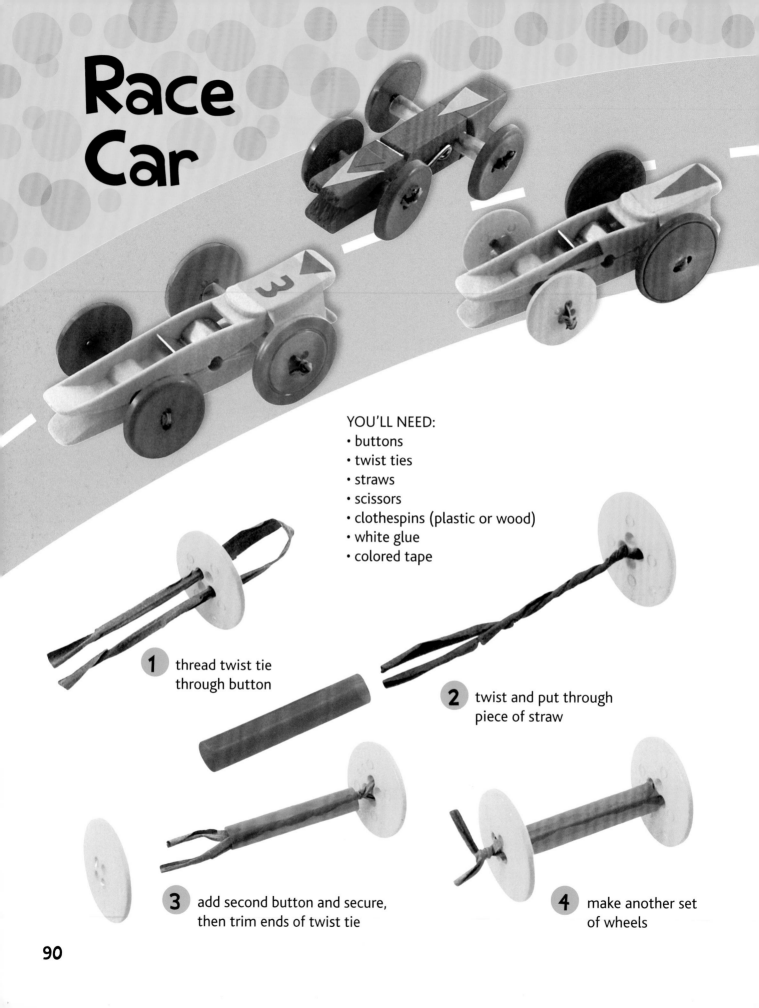

YOU'LL NEED:
- buttons
- twist ties
- straws
- scissors
- clothespins (plastic or wood)
- white glue
- colored tape

1 thread twist tie through button

2 twist and put through piece of straw

3 add second button and secure, then trim ends of twist tie

4 make another set of wheels

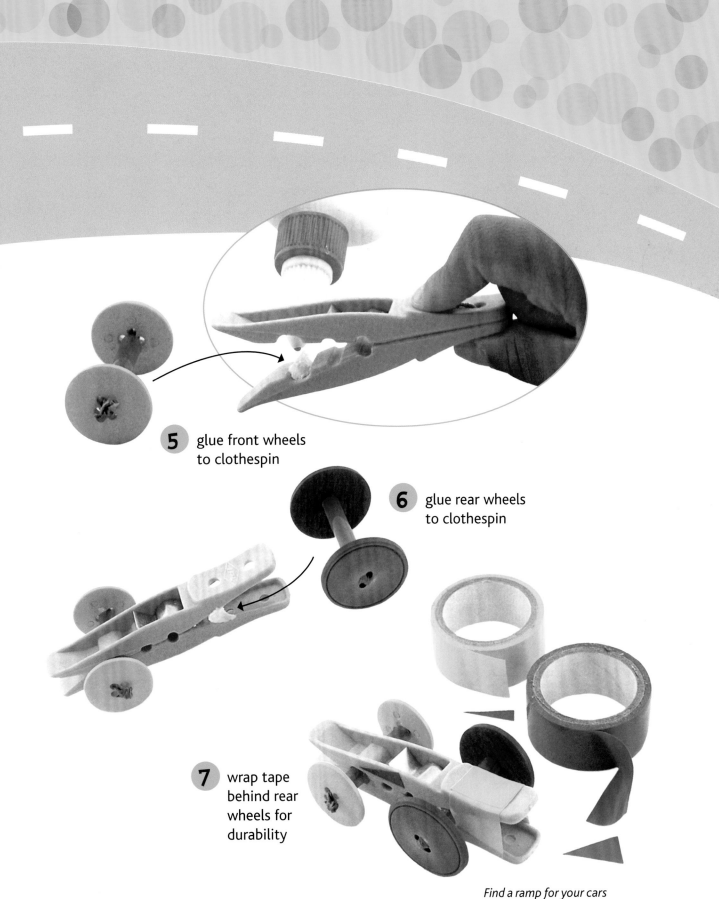

5   glue front wheels to clothespin

6   glue rear wheels to clothespin

7   wrap tape behind rear wheels for durability

Find a ramp for your cars on page 99.

Eensy-Weensy People

decorate as you like

YOU'LL NEED:
- extra-long twist ties
- scissors
- embroidery floss
- white glue
- acrylic paint
- toothpicks

1 cut twist tie in half for arms

2 bend another twist tie for body

3 add arms

4 twist

5 leave top loop to attach hair

6 glue ends of floss and wrap tightly

7 glue both ends of floss for each color

8 thread floss through loop and knot to create hair

9 paint details and fold ends up for feet

Woo-hoooo! Let's play!

Turn the page to make furniture for your people.

Foam Furniture

YOU'LL NEED:
- sponges
- scissors
- aluminum foil
- white glue

decorate as you like

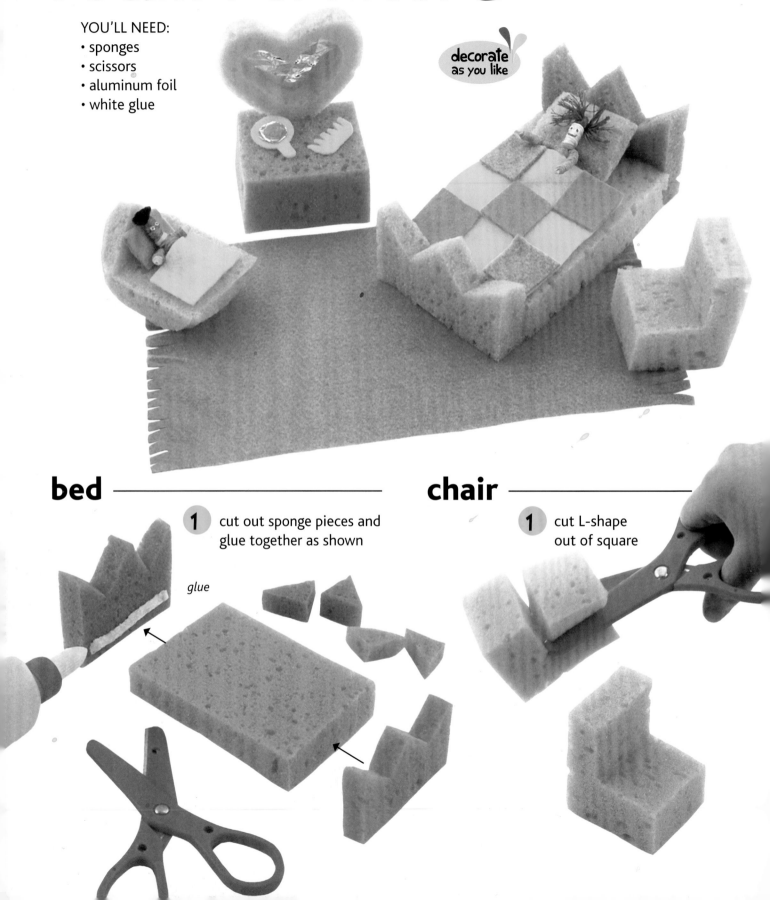

bed

1 cut out sponge pieces and glue together as shown

glue

chair

1 cut L-shape out of square

vanity

1 cut heart shape and remove center as shown

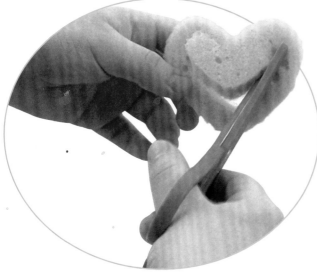

2 create mirror from aluminum foil and glue to back of heart shape frame

glue

3 glue mirror onto base

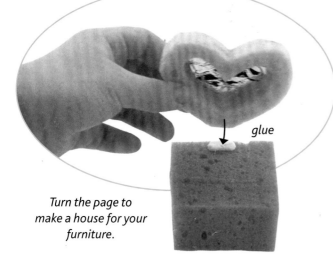

glue

Turn the page to make a house for your furniture.

cradle

1 cut L-shape out of square

2 trim back into triangle shape

3 trim into rounded shape as shown

Happy House

YOU'LL NEED:
- shoe box with lid
- pencil
- scissors
- bristol board
- clear tape
- small boxes
- colored paper
- white glue
- straw
- fabric scraps

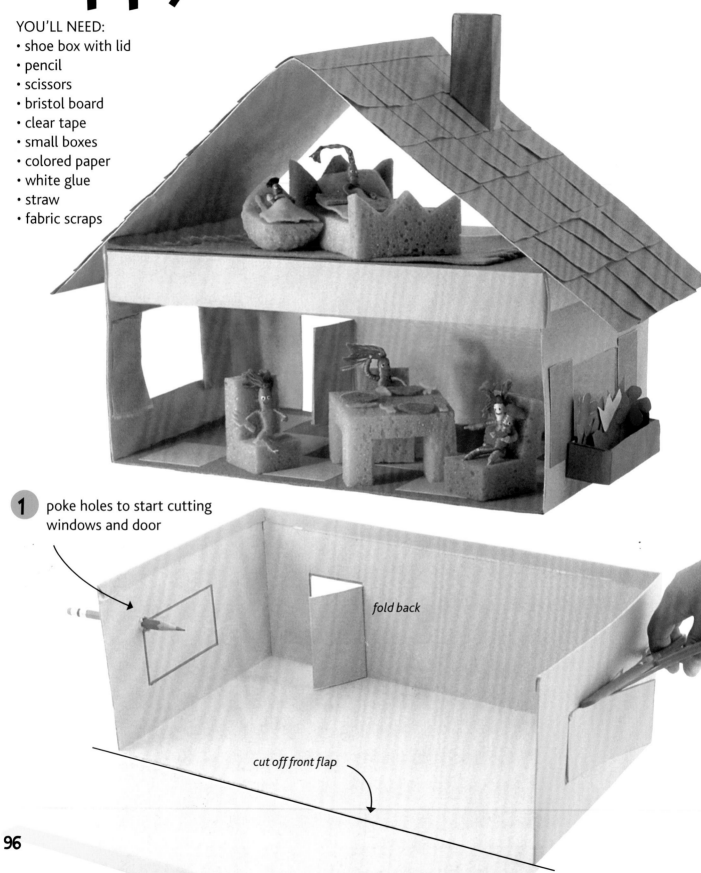

1 poke holes to start cutting windows and door

fold back

cut off front flap

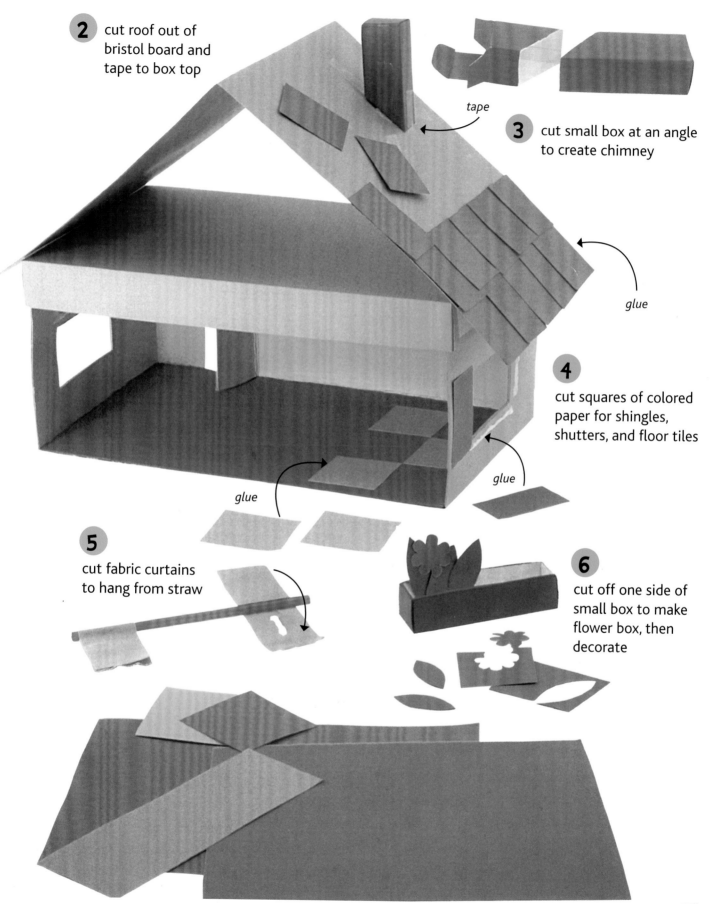

2 cut roof out of bristol board and tape to box top

tape

3 cut small box at an angle to create chimney

glue

4 cut squares of colored paper for shingles, shutters, and floor tiles

glue

glue

5 cut fabric curtains to hang from straw

6 cut off one side of small box to make flower box, then decorate

Build-a-Toy Set

decorate as you like

YOU'LL NEED:
- cardboard boxes
- scissors
- paper towel tubes
- toilet paper tubes
- tempera paint
- paintbrush
- colored construction paper
- pencil
- white glue

1 cut circles, rectangles, and triangles out of cardboard boxes

2 cut 2 slits into each tube end

3 paint shapes and tubes

4 connect shapes and tubes to build these toys and more

Find painting tips on page 7.

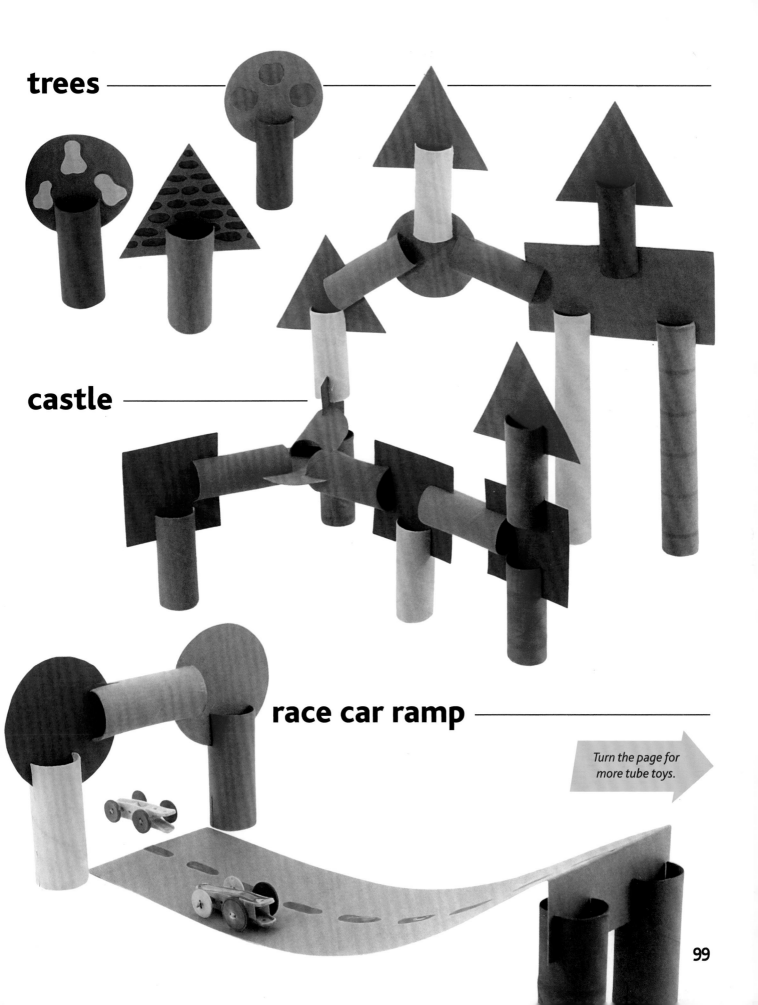

trees

castle

race car ramp

Turn the page for more tube toys.

99

log cabin

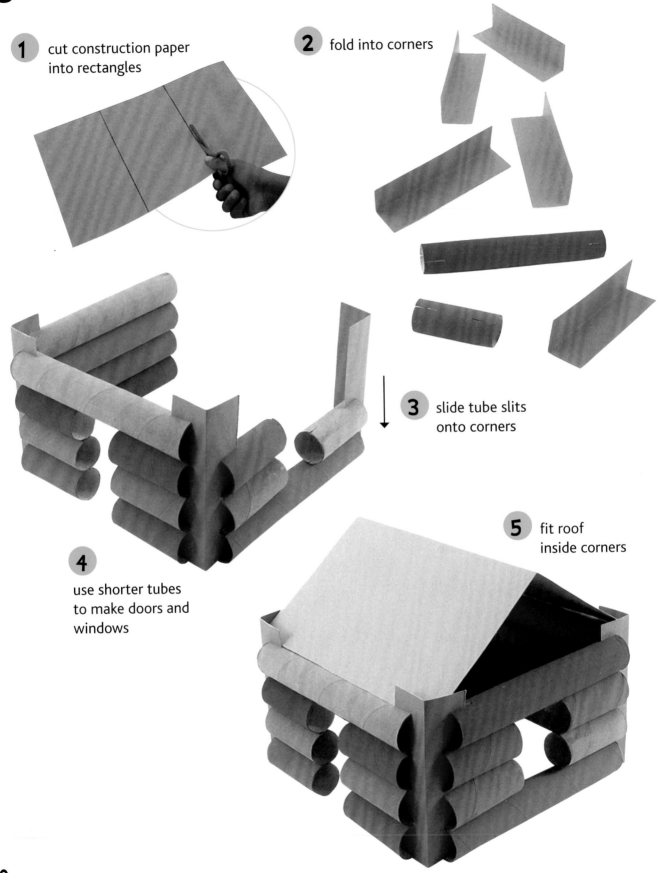

1 cut construction paper into rectangles

2 fold into corners

3 slide tube slits onto corners

4 use shorter tubes to make doors and windows

5 fit roof inside corners

horse

1 cut out head and tail pieces

Find pattern on page 145.

2 glue top parts of head pieces only

3 glue top parts of tail pieces only

4 cut mane and tail as shown

bend

5 slide on half of short tube for head

6 fit legs into tube slits

corral

horse jump

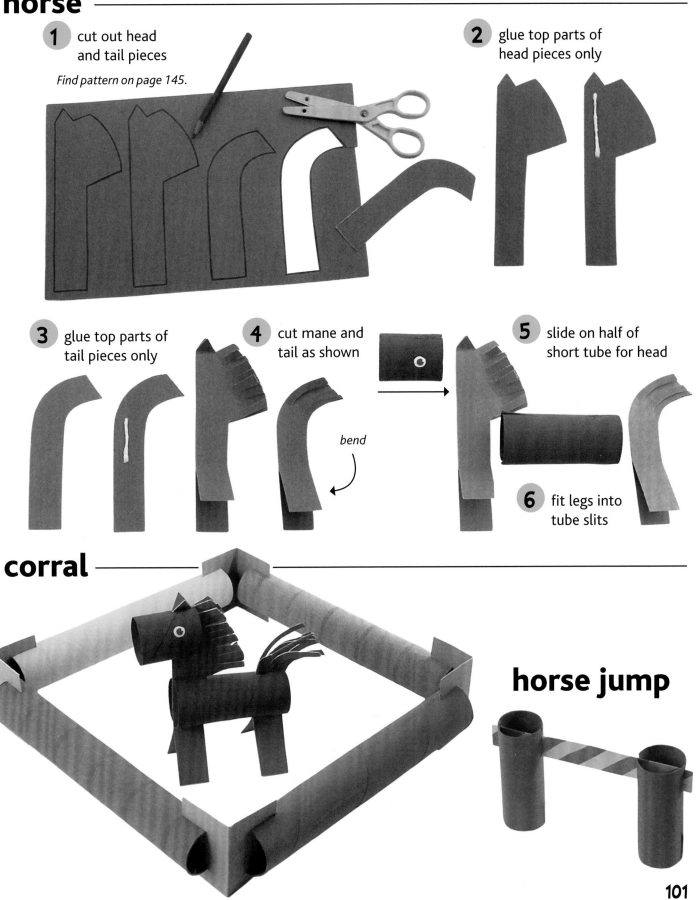

Flying Flapper

decorate as you like

YOU'LL NEED:
- construction paper
- pencil
- scissors
- stickers
- 13 to 20 feet (4 to 6 meters) heavy thread
- straw
- colored tape

1 fold paper in half and draw shape on one side

Find pattern on page 146.

2 cut through both halves

3 decorate both sides

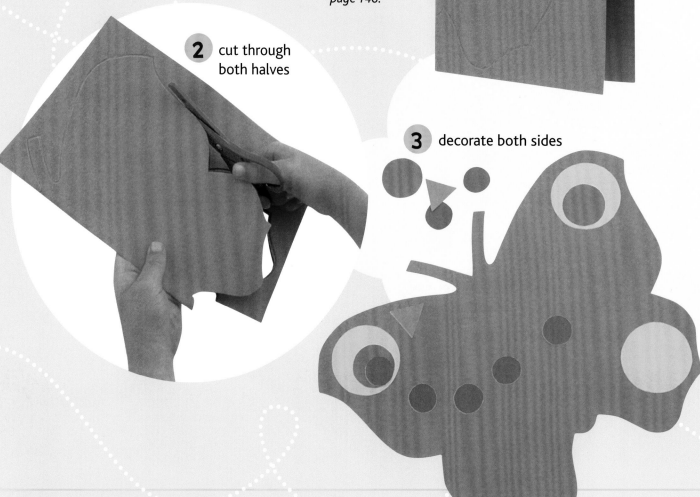

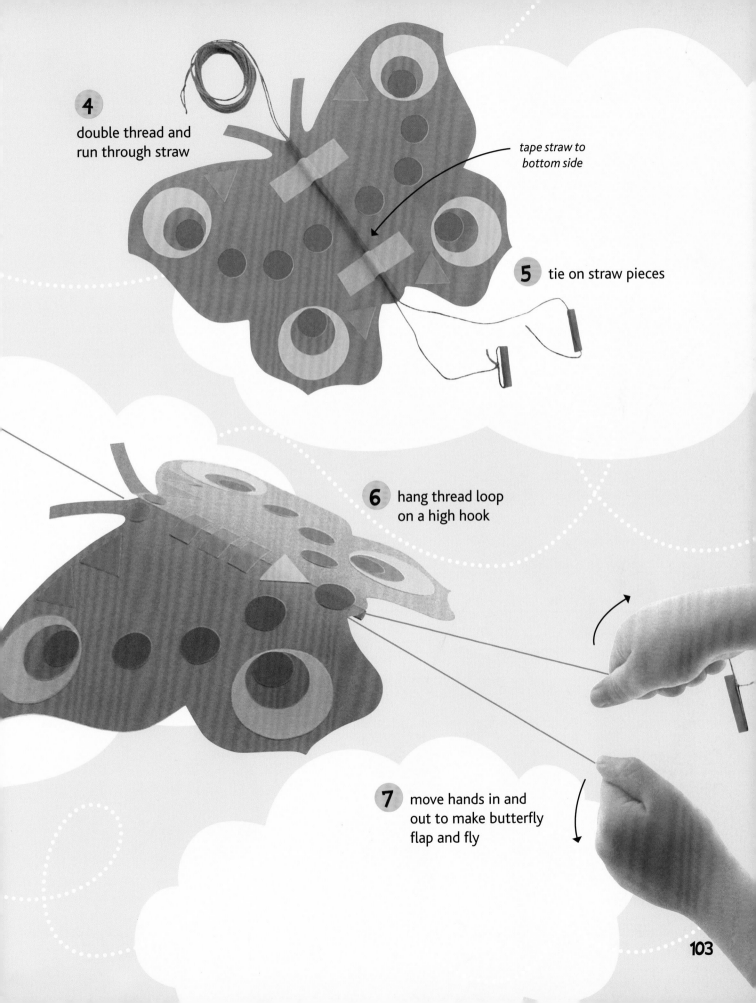

4 double thread and run through straw

tape straw to bottom side

5 tie on straw pieces

6 hang thread loop on a high hook

7 move hands in and out to make butterfly flap and fly

Bunny Buddy

ASK FOR ADULT HELP

YOU'LL NEED:
- sock
- scissors
- stuffing
- strong thread
- large needle
- googly eyes
- yarn
- button
- ribbon
- pompom

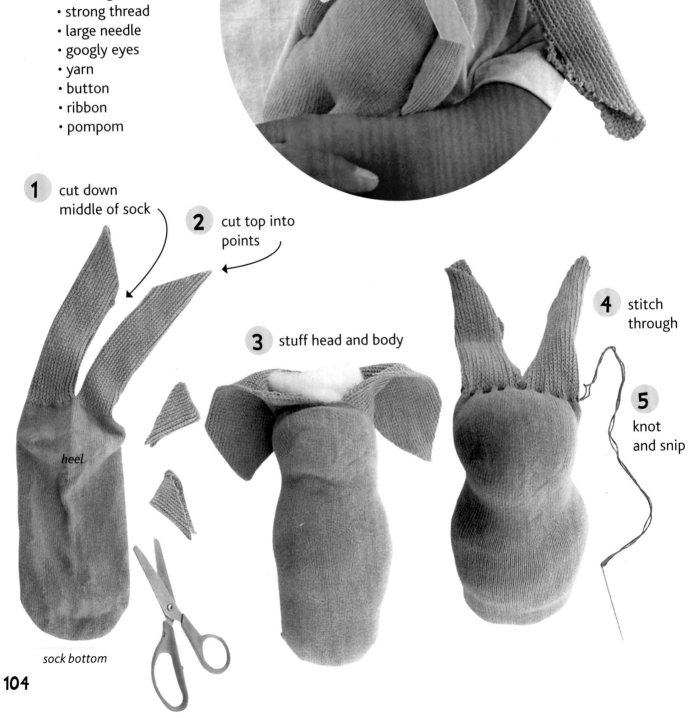

1 cut down middle of sock

2 cut top into points

heel

sock bottom

3 stuff head and body

4 stitch through

5 knot and snip

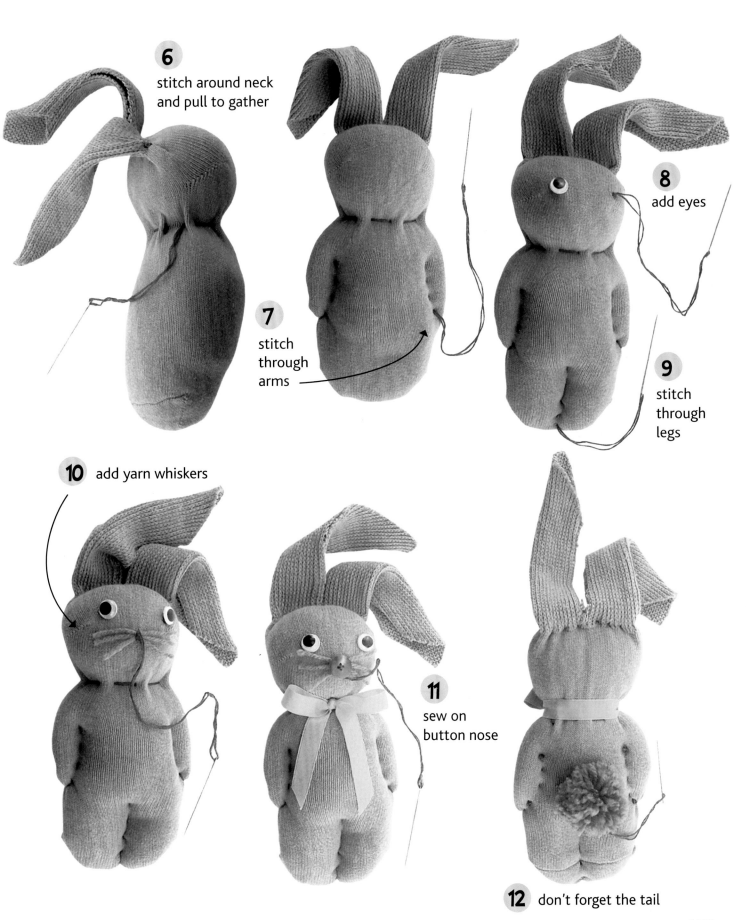

6 stitch around neck and pull to gather

7 stitch through arms

8 add eyes

9 stitch through legs

10 add yarn whiskers

11 sew on button nose

12 don't forget the tail

105

Mini-Messenger

I've got a message for you!

YOU'LL NEED:
- toilet paper tube
- tissue paper
- tape
- colored paper
- white glue
- scissors
- bristol board
- small box
- paint
- paintbrush
- hole punch
- googly eyes
- markers
- pencil
- yarn
- scrap paper

1 crumple 1 piece tissue paper

2 fit in bottom of roll

tape to make bottom

3 cover roll with paper

glue

4 cut arms and legs out of bristol board

arms

legs

glue

5 snip to make fingers to hold message

106

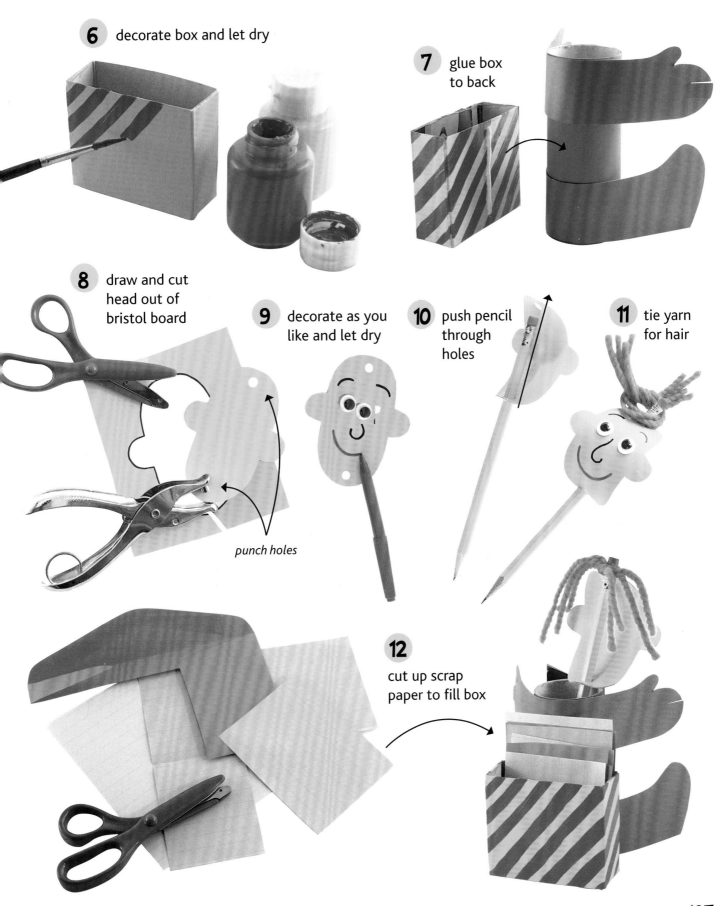

6 decorate box and let dry

7 glue box to back

8 draw and cut head out of bristol board

9 decorate as you like and let dry

10 push pencil through holes

11 tie yarn for hair

punch holes

12 cut up scrap paper to fill box

Dinosaur Puzzle

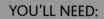

YOU'LL NEED:
- tracing paper
- markers
- scissors
- thin foam
- bristol board
- white glue
- acrylic or fabric paint
- paintbrush

Trace the frame and shapes from the pattern on page 148 or make your own.

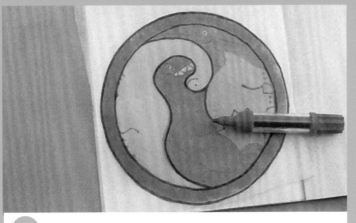

1 draw shapes and frame onto tracing paper

2 cut out paper shapes and frame

3 trace frame onto foam

4 trace shapes onto foam

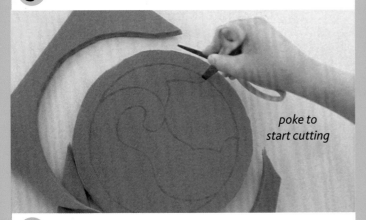

poke to start cutting

5 cut shapes out of foam

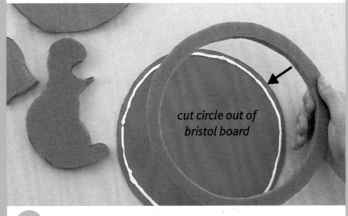

cut circle out of bristol board

6 glue frame to bristol board circle

7 paint pieces and let dry

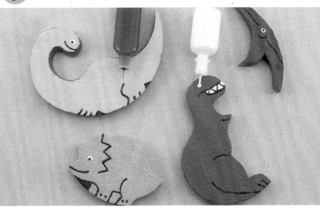

8 paint details

Suncatcher

ASK FOR ADULT HELP

A suncatcher made from colored tissue paper and hung in a window looks like stained glass. Stained glass is like a painting made of light. Pieces of colored glass are put together with metal strips in between. Sunlight shines through the glass, making it glow with light and color.

YOU'LL NEED:
- cardboard
- pencil
- scissors
- clear plastic wrap
- clear tape
- colored tissue paper
- colored tape
- hole punch
- yarn

1 draw shape on cardboard and cut out

2 cut out center, leaving frame around outside

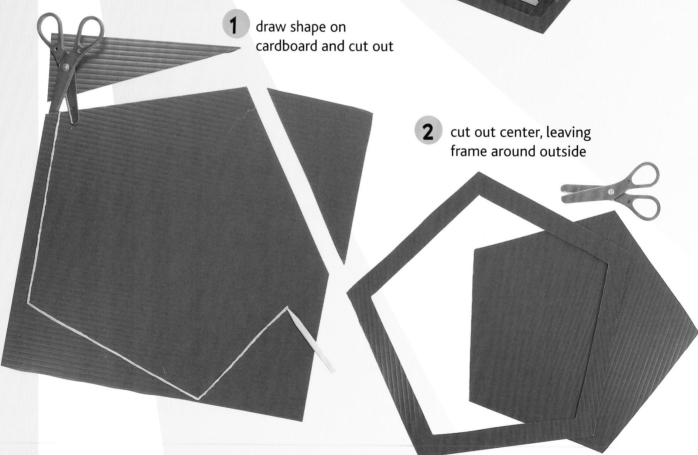

3 stretch plastic wrap over frame and tape down as shown

back

4 trim plastic wrap a bit bigger than inside of frame

5 cut pieces of tissue paper

6 use clear tape to tape pieces together over plastic wrap

front

7 use colored tape to tape over seams where pieces meet

8 punch hole and thread yarn through

9 knot ends and hang

Little Gallery

An art gallery is a place to show art, sometimes in special shows called exhibits. An exhibit might show the work of one artist, or art that has to do with a certain subject or theme. What theme do you think is shown here?

gallery

YOU'LL NEED:
- shoe box
- scissors
- light colored paint
- paintbrush

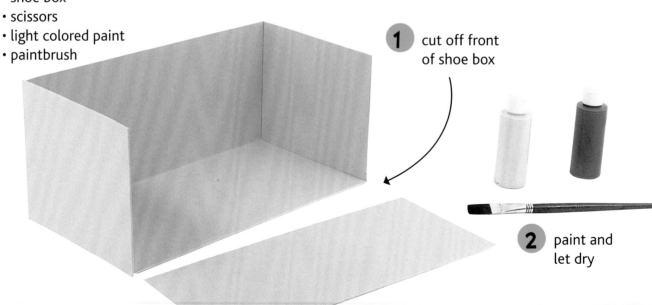

1 cut off front of shoe box

2 paint and let dry

frame

YOU'LL NEED:
- mini-painting
- scissors
- construction paper
- white glue

1 trim edges of painting

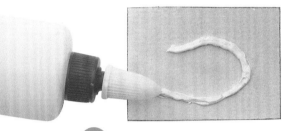

2 glue back

3 glue to piece of paper a little bigger than painting

easel

YOU'LL NEED:
- 2 drinking straws
- scissors
- tape

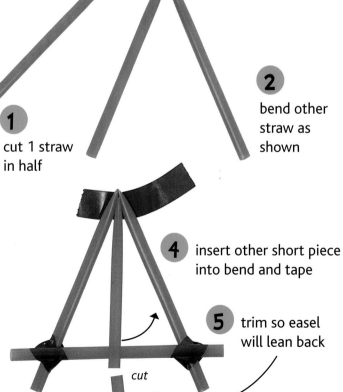

1 cut 1 straw in half

2 bend other straw as shown

3 tape 1 short piece across as shown

4 insert other short piece into bend and tape

5 trim so easel will lean back

cut

Toy Box

YOU'LL NEED:
- cardboard box with hinged lid
- colored paper
- white glue that dries clear
- water
- bowl
- pencil
- hole punch
- string
- large button

1 tear strips of colored paper

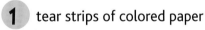

2 mix together equal parts white glue and water

3 dip paper pieces into mixture and smooth onto box, then let dry overnight

5 punch holes on top and front of box near edge

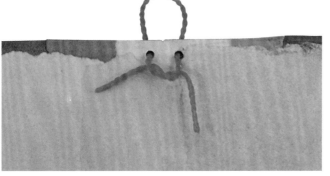

6 tie string to make loop on top of box lid

7 thread button on another piece of string

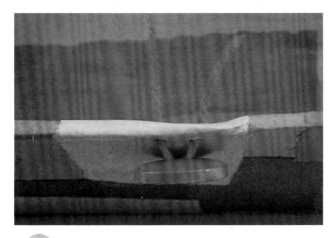

8 attach button to outside of box front

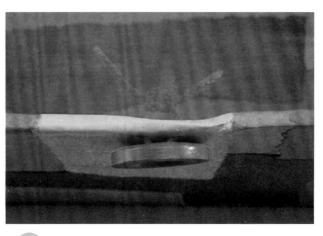

9 tie down

115

WORLD'S BEST BROTHER

116

Let's Make Games

Tangle

YOU'LL NEED:
- 2 milk or juice cartons
- scissors
- masking tape
- six colors of construction paper
- pencil
- white glue

1 cut 2 square boxes from carton bottoms

2 cut slit at 1 corner of each box

3 push boxes together

4 tape slit shut

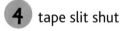

5 trace box shape onto paper

6 cut 5 traced squares of each color

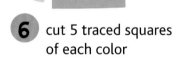

7 glue a different color on each side of box to make chooser

8 gather 4 paper squares of each color

how to play
- 2 to 6 can play. Find a clear space on a rug.
- Scatter paper squares on the rug.
- Roll the chooser. The color on top is your color.
- Try to touch all the paper squares of your color at once, using your hands and feet.
- Add your own rules. Try not to get too tangled!

118

Owl Eyes

ASK FOR ADULT HELP

YOU'LL NEED:
- small box
- paper
- pencil
- scissors
- markers
- white glue
- foam tray
- hole punch
- 6 beads
- plastic wrap
- tape

1 trace box onto paper

cut out

2 draw owls on paper

cut out

3 glue paper to foam tray

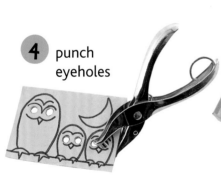

4 punch eyeholes

5 glue into box and let dry

6 put beads in box

7 stretch wrap over box

8 tape around edges of wrap and trim

how to play

- 1 person can play.
- Shake box gently to roll beads into eyeholes.

Squishers

YOU'LL NEED:
- large balloons
- funnel
- fine sand or flour
- spoon
- pencil

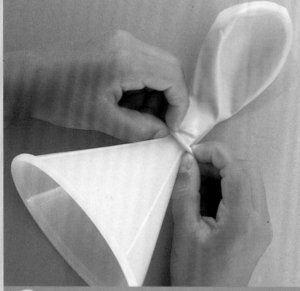

1 pull balloon onto funnel

2 spoon in sand or flour to fill balloon

3 poke gently with pencil

4 tap filling down and squish balloon to get rid of air

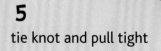

5 tie knot and pull tight

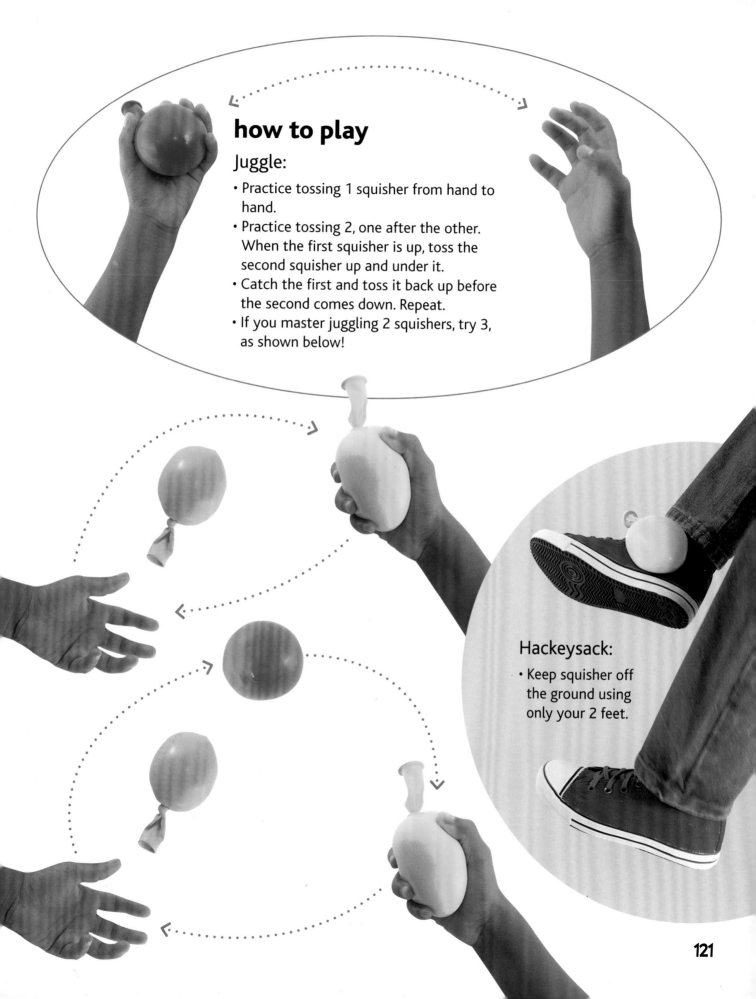

how to play

Juggle:

- Practice tossing 1 squisher from hand to hand.
- Practice tossing 2, one after the other. When the first squisher is up, toss the second squisher up and under it.
- Catch the first and toss it back up before the second comes down. Repeat.
- If you master juggling 2 squishers, try 3, as shown below!

Hackeysack:

- Keep squisher off the ground using only your 2 feet.

Cat and Mouse

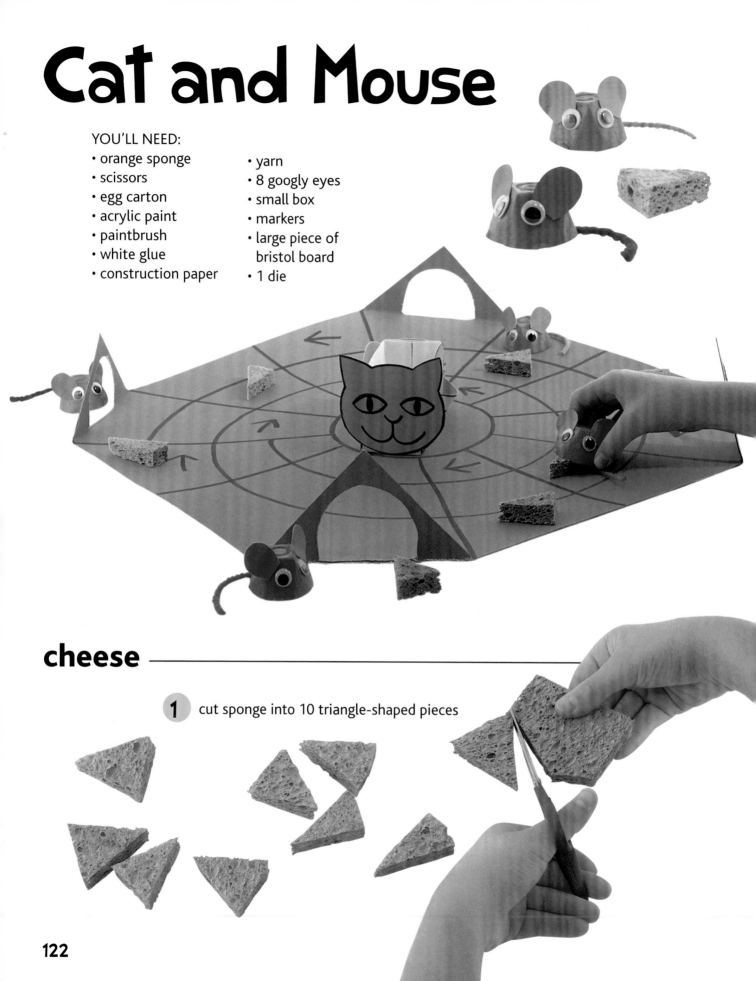

YOU'LL NEED:
- orange sponge
- scissors
- egg carton
- acrylic paint
- paintbrush
- white glue
- construction paper
- yarn
- 8 googly eyes
- small box
- markers
- large piece of bristol board
- 1 die

cheese

1 cut sponge into 10 triangle-shaped pieces

122

mice

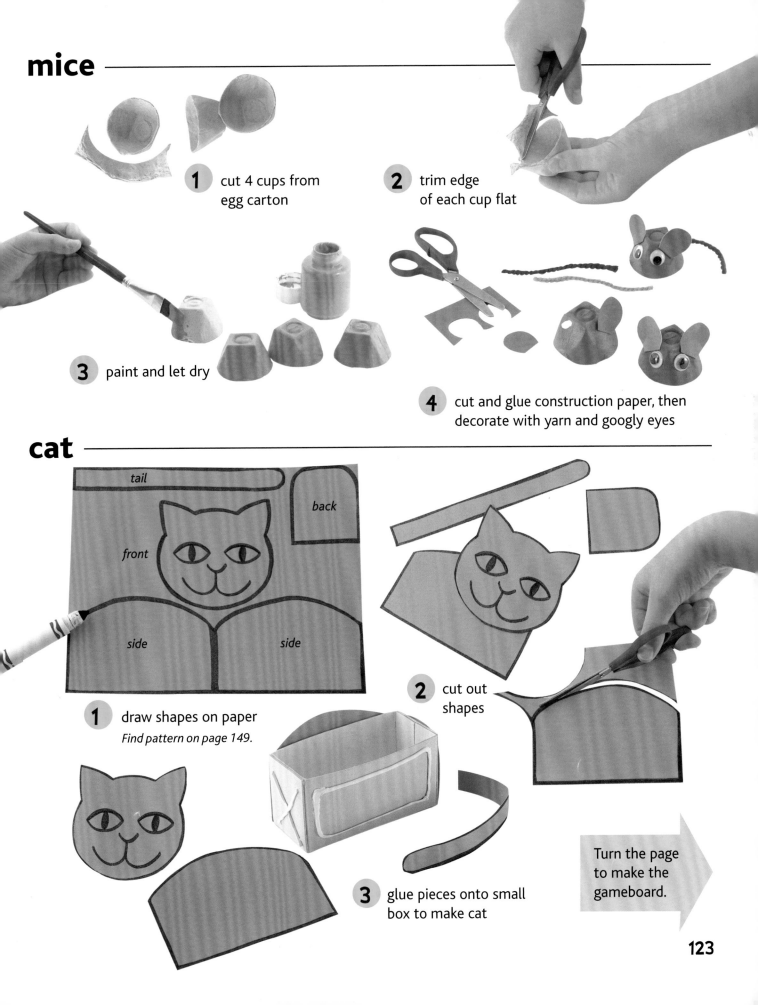

1 cut 4 cups from egg carton

2 trim edge of each cup flat

3 paint and let dry

4 cut and glue construction paper, then decorate with yarn and googly eyes

cat

tail

back

front

side   side

1 draw shapes on paper
Find pattern on page 149.

2 cut out shapes

3 glue pieces onto small box to make cat

Turn the page to make the gameboard.

123

gameboard

1 cut one end off bristol board to make it square

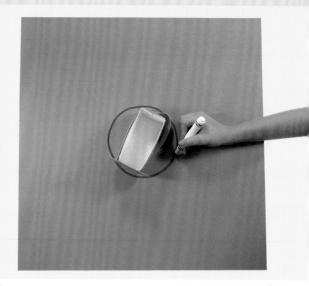

2 draw a circle big enough for the cat

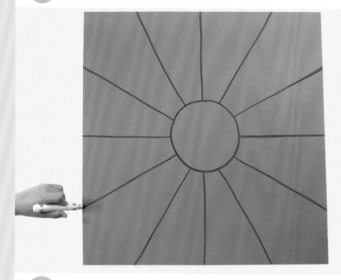

3 draw 12 lines as shown

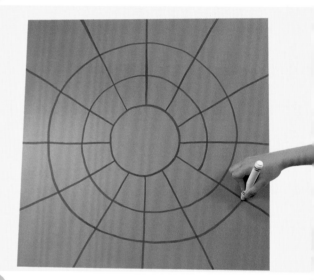

4 draw a spiral as shown

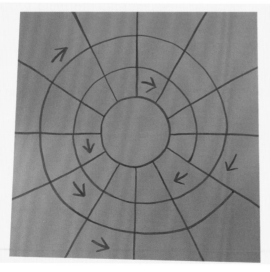

5 draw arrows as shown

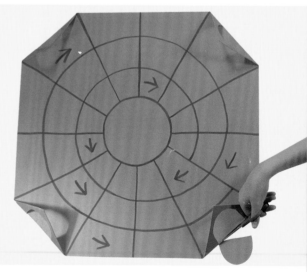

6 fold up corners and cut out mouse holes

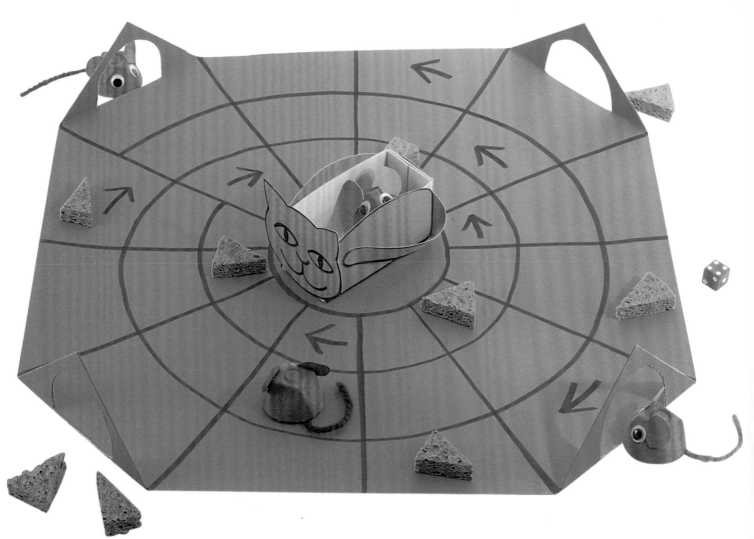

how to play

- 2 or more play this cooperative game.

- Scatter cheese on the board. Place the cat in the middle. Mice start at the mouse holes. Mice that land in the row of spaces directly in front of the cat are caught and go in the cat.
- Take turns rolling the die. Choose any mouse and move along the spiral toward the center. If a mouse reaches the center, it turns around and returns to its hole.
- When a mouse lands on the same square as a piece of cheese, it picks up the cheese and takes it back to its mouse hole. After a mouse gets a piece of cheese into its hole, it starts again. All moves are by roll of the die.
- When a mouse lands on an arrow, the cat turns one space in the direction of the arrow. Any mice now in the row of spaces directly in front of the cat are caught and go in the cat.
- Players plan together to outsmart the cat! Try to get as many mice and pieces of cheese as you can safely back into the mouse holes.

Hatching Egg

YOU'LL NEED:
- tracing paper
- 2 paper clips
- soft lead pencil
- scissors
- bristol board
- envelope

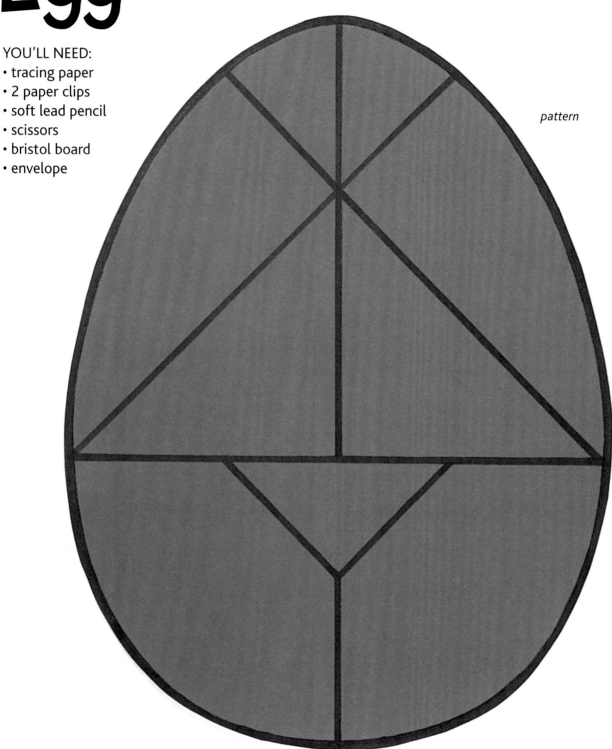

pattern

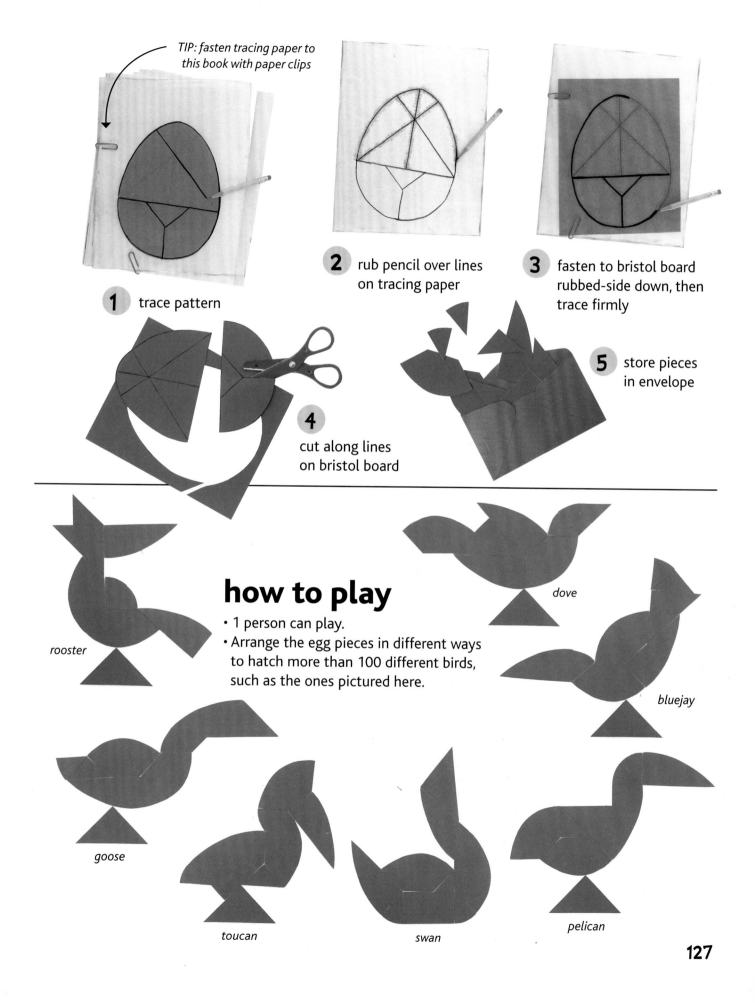

TIP: fasten tracing paper to this book with paper clips

1 trace pattern

2 rub pencil over lines on tracing paper

3 fasten to bristol board rubbed-side down, then trace firmly

4 cut along lines on bristol board

5 store pieces in envelope

how to play
- 1 person can play.
- Arrange the egg pieces in different ways to hatch more than 100 different birds, such as the ones pictured here.

rooster

dove

bluejay

goose

toucan

swan

pelican

Monkey Race

Find pattern on page 147.

YOU'LL NEED:
- tracing paper
- pencil
- scissors
- bristol board
- crayons
- straw
- tape
- stapler
- yarn
- paper towel tube

1 draw pattern onto tracing paper

2 cut out

3 trace outline onto bristol board

4 cut out and decorate

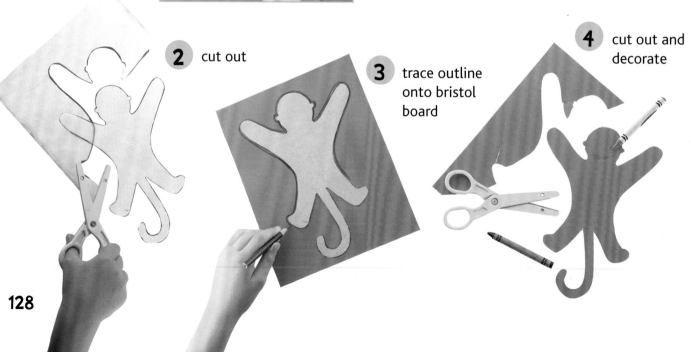

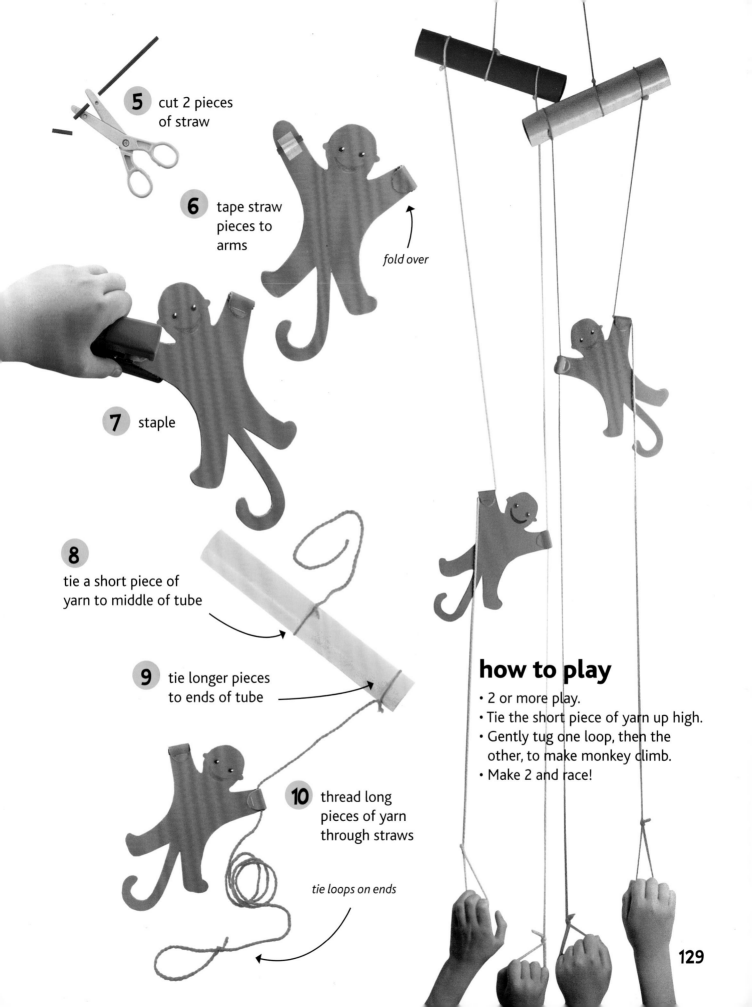

5 cut 2 pieces of straw

6 tape straw pieces to arms

fold over

7 staple

8 tie a short piece of yarn to middle of tube

9 tie longer pieces to ends of tube

10 thread long pieces of yarn through straws

tie loops on ends

how to play

- 2 or more play.
- Tie the short piece of yarn up high.
- Gently tug one loop, then the other, to make monkey climb.
- Make 2 and race!

129

Mini Golf

decorate as you like

golf club

YOU'LL NEED:
- long paper tube
- scissors
- short paper tube
- stapler
- acrylic paint
- paintbrush

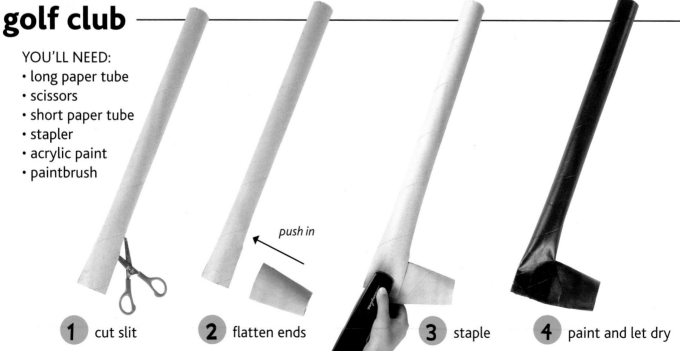

push in

1 cut slit

2 flatten ends

3 staple

4 paint and let dry

cup

YOU'LL NEED:
- bristol board
- scissors
- construction paper
- marker
- bendable straw
- tape

1 cut circle from bristol board

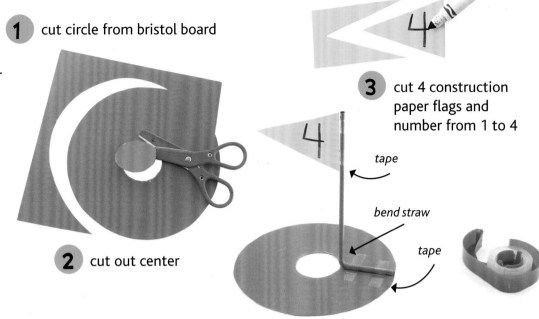

2 cut out center

3 cut 4 construction paper flags and number from 1 to 4

tape

bend straw

tape

tee

YOU'LL NEED:
- bristol board
- scissors
- egg carton
- tape
- acrylic paint
- paintbrush

1 cut bristol board circle

2 cut and trim an egg cup

tape

3 decorate and let dry

Turn the page to make the hazards.

how to play

- 2 or more play. Find a clear space for playing.
- Set up course: 1 tee, 1 hazard, and 1 cup for each hole.
- Start by putting a small ball on the first tee. Hit the ball with the golf club. Try to hit it through the hazard and then into the cup with as few swings as possible.
- Your score is the number of hits it takes to get the ball in the cup.
- After everyone plays all 4 holes, total each player's score. The lowest total score wins.

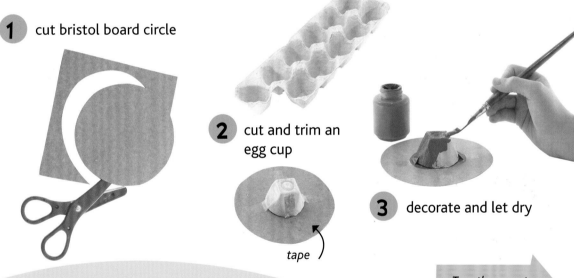

HAZARDS

YOU'LL NEED:
- 4 cardboard boxes
- pencil
- scissors
- bristol board
- glue or tape
- acrylic paint and brush
- paper tube

crocodile

1 draw lines and cut as shown

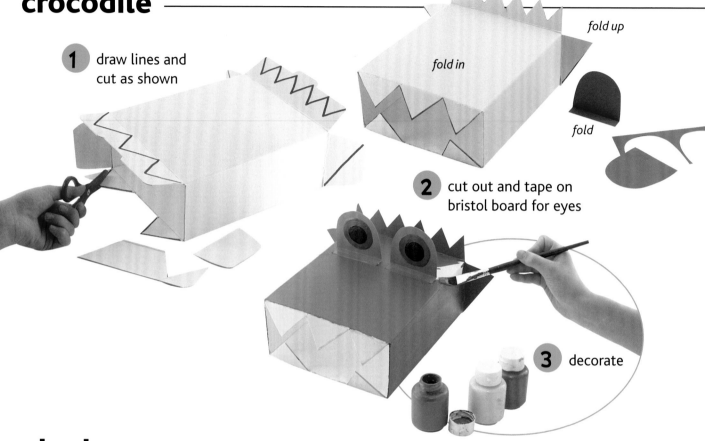

fold up

fold in

fold

2 cut out and tape on bristol board for eyes

3 decorate

elephant

1 draw arch on both sides of box and cut out

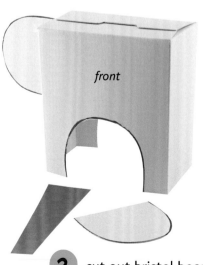

front

2 cut out bristol board ears and trunk, and tape on

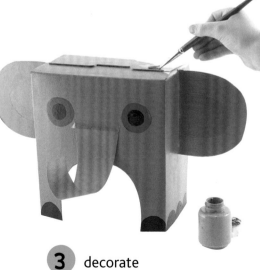

3 decorate

hippo

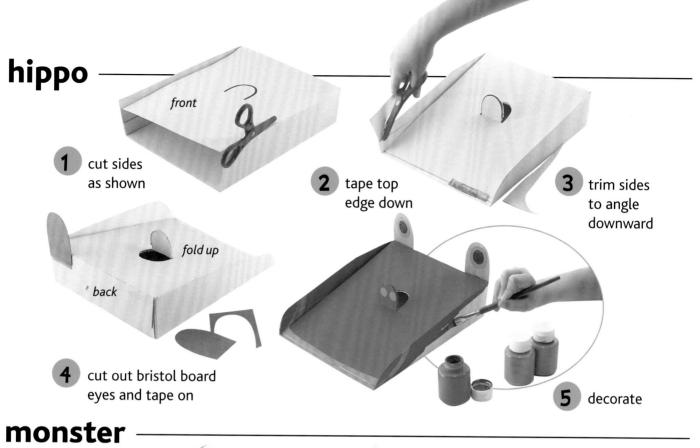

1 cut sides as shown

front

2 tape top edge down

3 trim sides to angle downward

back

fold up

4 cut out bristol board eyes and tape on

5 decorate

monster

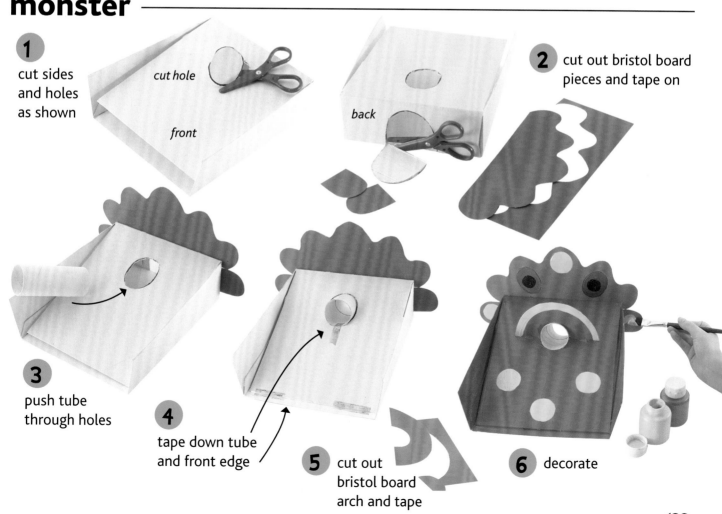

1 cut sides and holes as shown

cut hole

front

back

2 cut out bristol board pieces and tape on

3 push tube through holes

4 tape down tube and front edge

5 cut out bristol board arch and tape

6 decorate

Pinball Bowl

YOU'LL NEED:
- 5 short tubes
- acrylic paint
- paintbrush
- fat paper tube
- thin paper tube
- hole punch
- masking tape
- rubber bands
- yarn
- aluminum foil

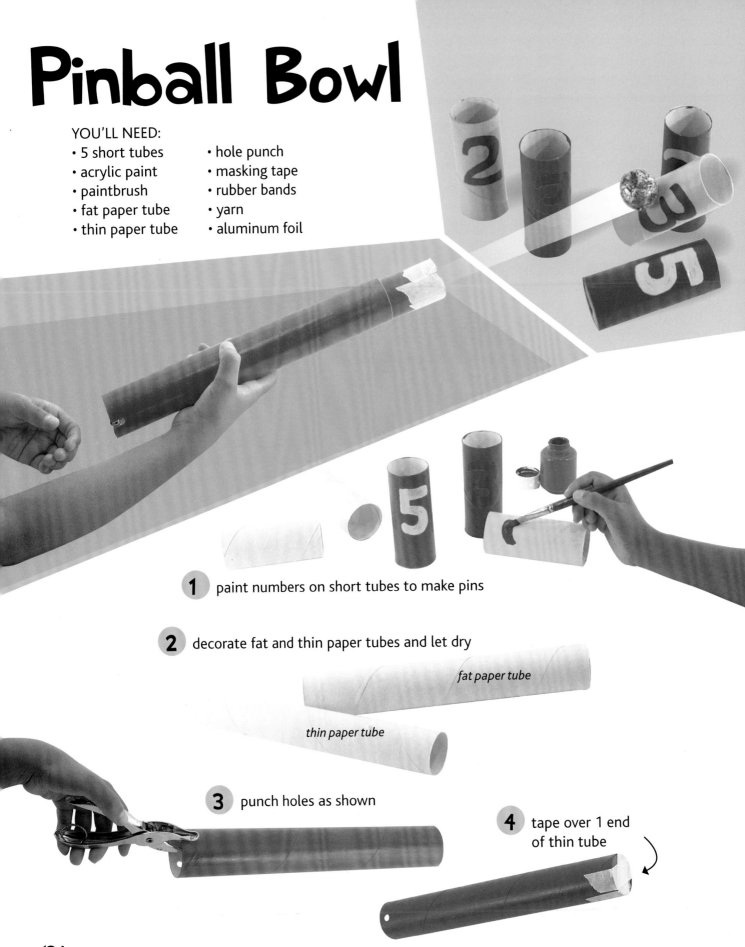

1. paint numbers on short tubes to make pins

2. decorate fat and thin paper tubes and let dry

   fat paper tube

   thin paper tube

3. punch holes as shown

4. tape over 1 end of thin tube

5 attach rubber bands to fat tube by pulling one end through the other

6 put thin tube inside

7 push rubber bands through holes in thin tube

8 tie rubber bands together with yarn

9 crumple aluminum foil into balls

10 load foil ball

how to play

- 2 or more play. Find a clear space for playing.
- Arrange pins in a V-shape. Load ball, pull back the inside tube, and let go to shoot. Add up the points printed on the pins you've knocked down.
- The player with the most points wins.

Six-Man Morris

YOU'LL NEED:
- colored paper
- scissors
- white glue
- cardboard
- marker
- 16 star stickers
- 6 buttons
- 6 bottle caps

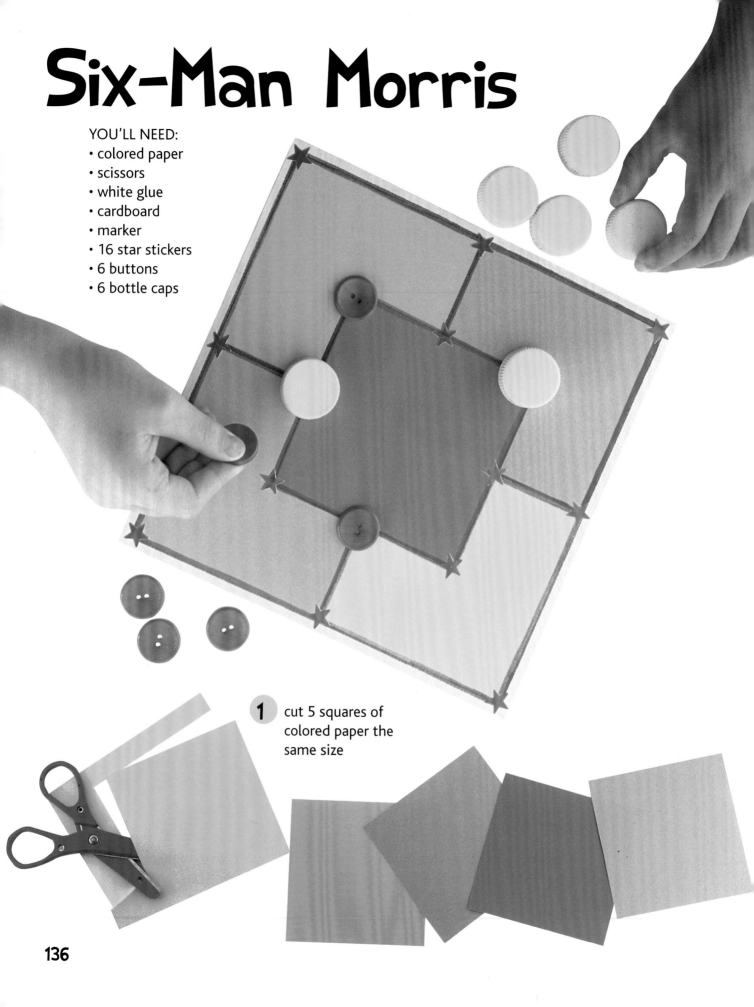

1 cut 5 squares of colored paper the same size

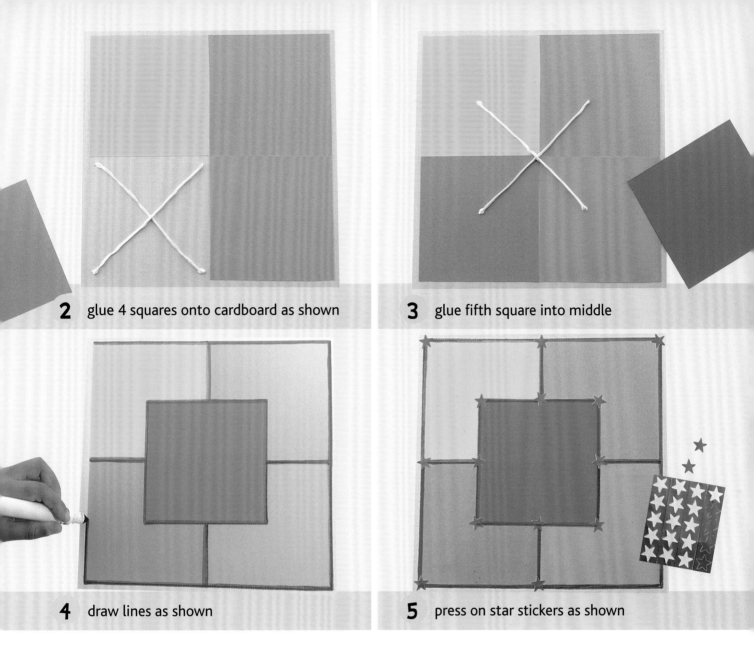

2 glue 4 squares onto cardboard as shown

3 glue fifth square into middle

4 draw lines as shown

5 press on star stickers as shown

how to play

- 2 people play. The best way to learn this game is to play it!
- Each player has either 6 buttons or 6 bottle caps as playing pieces.
- Start by placing your pieces on uncovered stars. Take turns placing 1 piece on the board at a time.
- Throughout the game, try to get 3 pieces in a row along a line. These will be "safe." Any time you get a safe row of 3 on the board, you can take 1 of the other player's pieces, as long as it is not in a safe row.
- When a piece is taken, it is out of play. Once all your pieces are on the board, take turns moving pieces, one at a time. A piece can move along any line to an uncovered star next to it. (You can't make the same row of three more than once.)
- When you have only 3 pieces left, you can jump to any uncovered star.
- You win when the other player has only 2 pieces left, or when you have blocked all the other player's moves.

X Treasure Hunt

ASK AN ADULT BEFORE YOU DIG

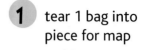

YOU'LL NEED:
- 2 brown paper bags
- soil
- water
- bowl
- plastic bag
- pencil crayons
- scissors
- envelope
- tape
- treasure (candy, toys, books, etc.)
- aluminum foil
- toy shovel

1 tear 1 bag into piece for map

2 tear other bag into smaller pieces for clues

3 crinkle all pieces

4 smooth out flat

5 mix 2 spoonfuls of soil into bowl of water

6 dip paper into water and let dry on plastic bag

138

7 decide where to hide clues and treasure

8 draw treasure map

9 write and number clues

① Climb the stairs to where you sleep. On the floor you'll have to creep.

② Find the tree that has a split. Stand on your toes and reach for it.

③ Come out here to rest your feet. Look underneath this cosy red seat.

10 cut up map and put pieces in envelope with roll of tape

how to play

- 2 or more play: one treasure hider and one or more treasure hunters.
- Hide the treasure. If you want to bury it, wrap it in aluminum foil first.
- Hide the map and clues #2 and #3. Clue #1 will lead to the location of clue #2. Clue #2 will lead to clue #3. Clue #3 will lead to the map.
- Give clue #1 to the treasure hunters.
- The treasure hunters must find the clues in order, find the map, and then tape the map together. The map will lead the hunters to the treasure.

Trip Kit

ASK FOR ADULT HELP

YOU'LL NEED:
- shoe box with lid
- felt
- scissors
- white glue
- chalk
- fabric marker
- hole punch
- envelopes for storing pieces

1 cut felt to fit box lid

2 glue felt to box lid

glue

storyboard

1 draw shapes and cut from felt

2 arrange pieces on box lid to make pictures and stories

X's and O's

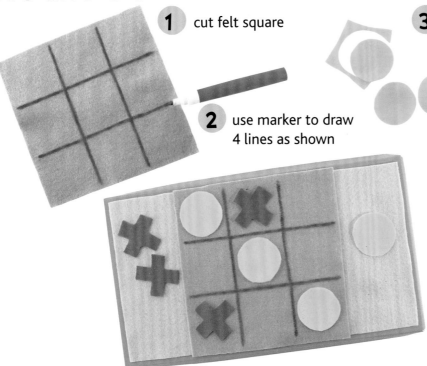

1 cut felt square

2 use marker to draw 4 lines as shown

3 cut 4 circles for O's, then cut 4 squares and remove corners for X's

how to play

- 2 people play.
- Place square on box lid.
- 1 player takes X's, the other player takes O's. Take turns putting your pieces on empty spaces.
- 3 in a row going any direction wins.

solitaire

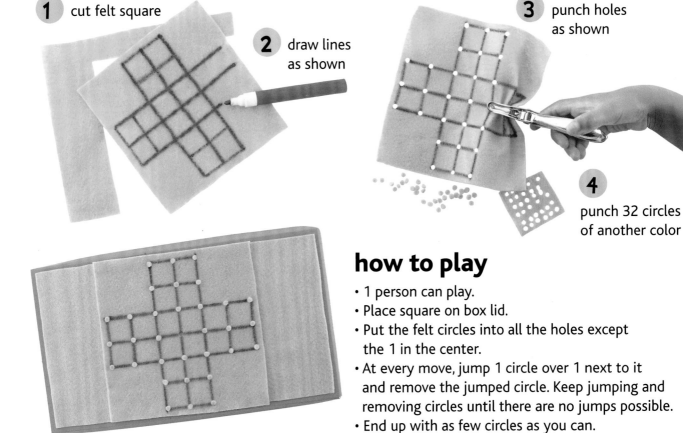

1 cut felt square

2 draw lines as shown

3 punch holes as shown

4 punch 32 circles of another color

how to play

- 1 person can play.
- Place square on box lid.
- Put the felt circles into all the holes except the 1 in the center.
- At every move, jump 1 circle over 1 next to it and remove the jumped circle. Keep jumping and removing circles until there are no jumps possible.
- End up with as few circles as you can.

Winning Trophy

ASK FOR ADULT HELP

YOU'LL NEED:
- corrugated cardboard
- scissors
- large plastic soda pop bottle
- masking tape
- aluminum foil
- clear tape
- stapler
- colored paper
- marker

WORLD'S BEST BROTHER

1 cut cardboard base

2 cut bottle in half

3 tape top of bottle to base with masking tape

4 gently line inside of bottle with foil

5 fold down and tape edges

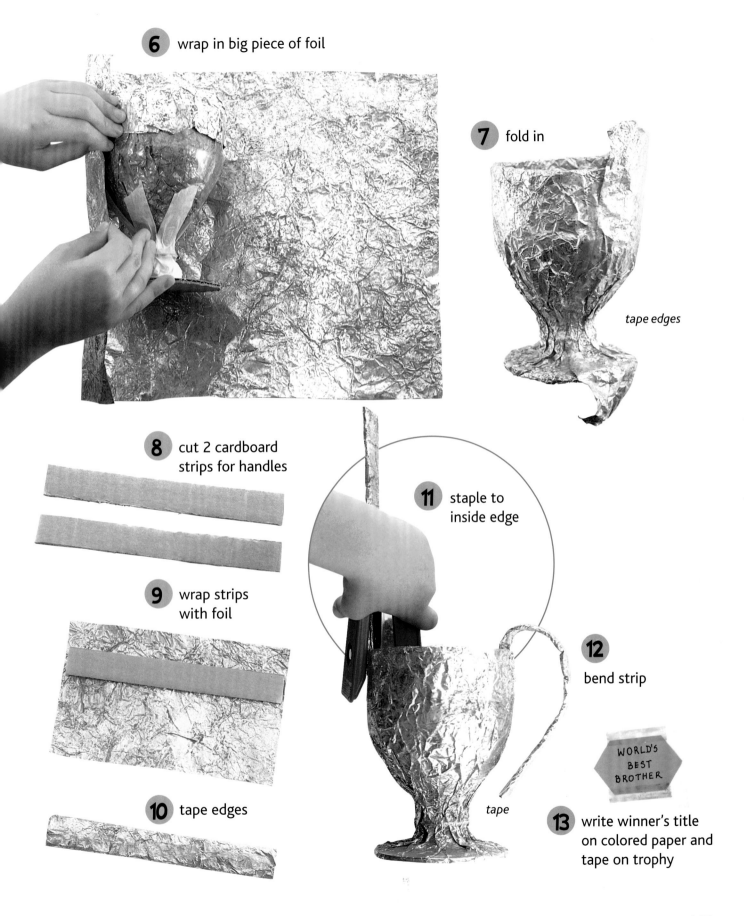

6 wrap in big piece of foil

7 fold in

tape edges

8 cut 2 cardboard strips for handles

9 wrap strips with foil

10 tape edges

11 staple to inside edge

12 bend strip

tape

WORLD'S BEST BROTHER

13 write winner's title on colored paper and tape on trophy

Patterns

HAND STAND
page 35

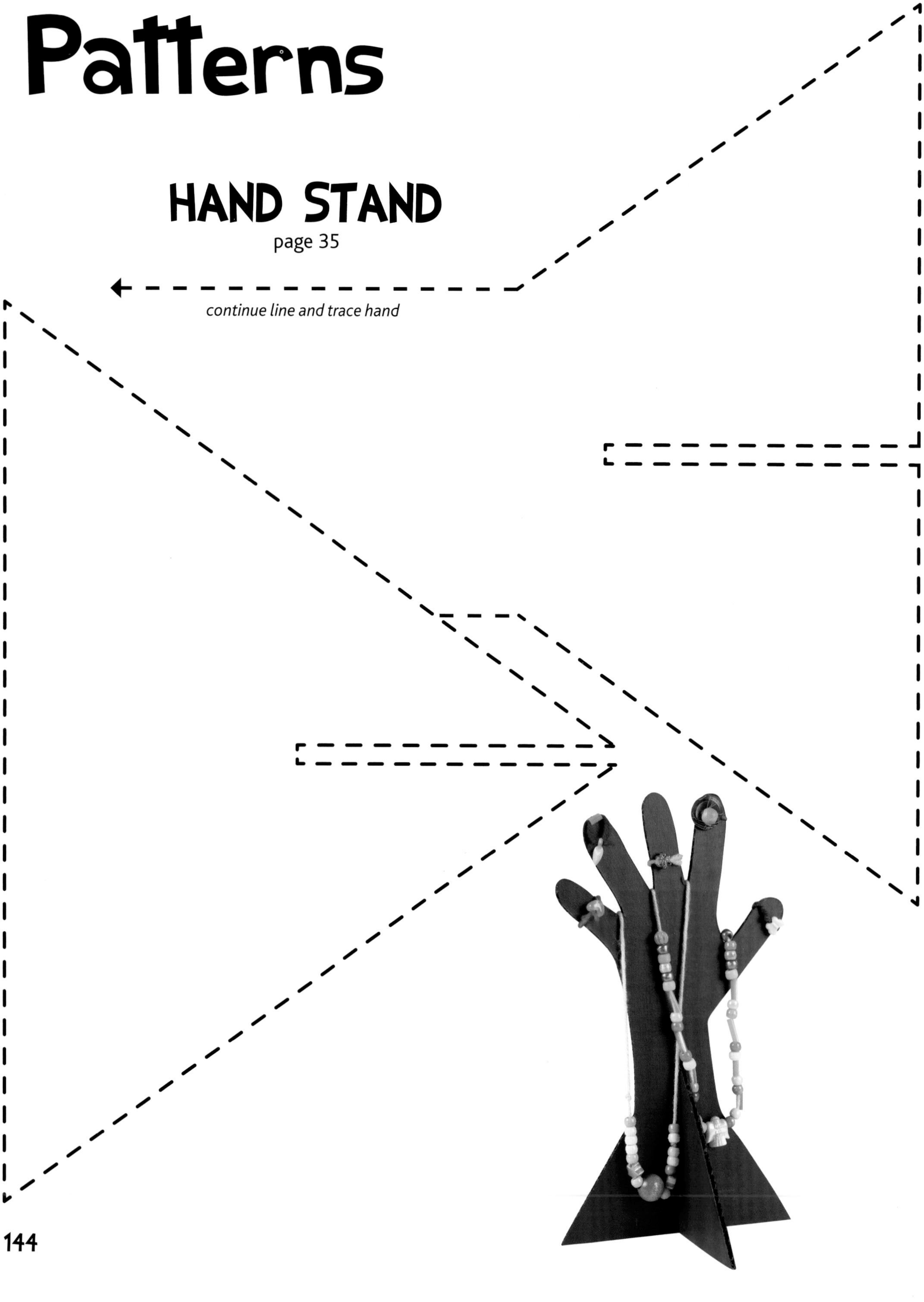

continue line and trace hand

144

HORSE

page 101

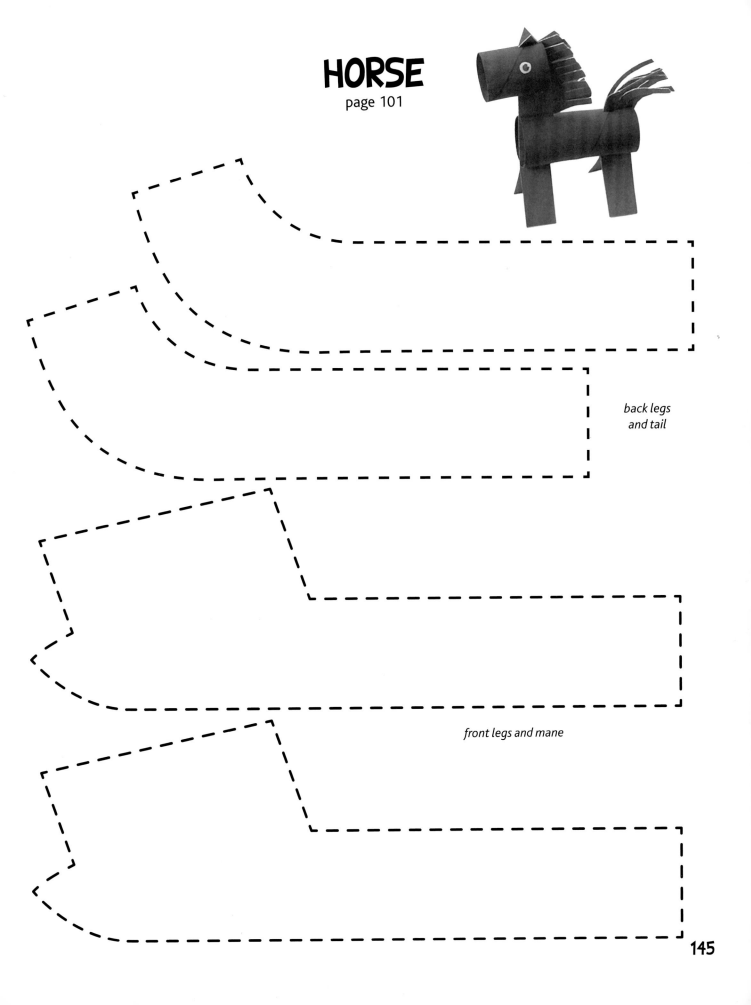

*back legs
and tail*

front legs and mane

145

FLYING FLAPPER

page 102

fold

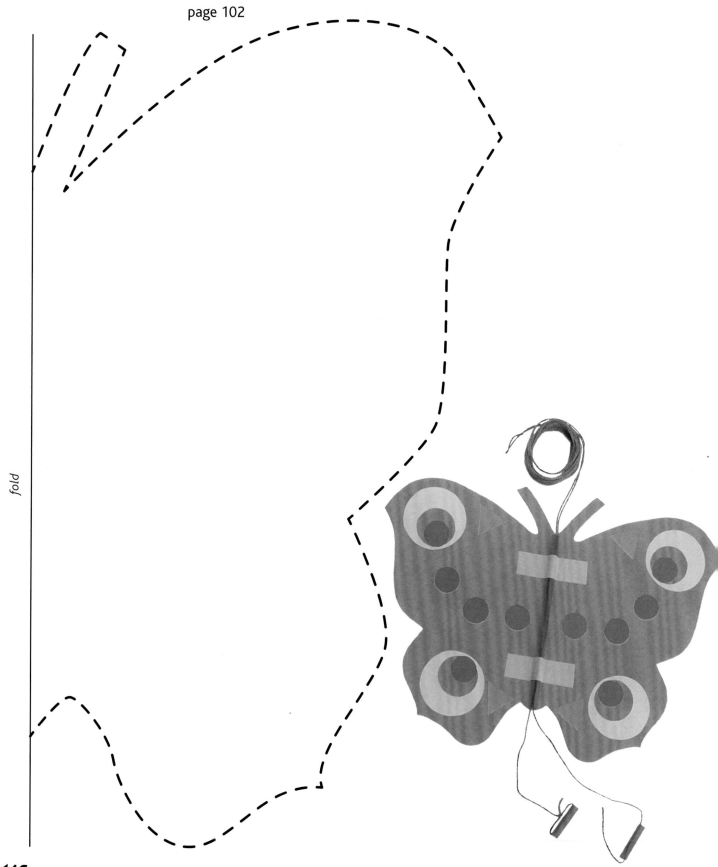

MONKEY RACE

page 128

fold

fold

DINOSAUR PUZZLE

page 108

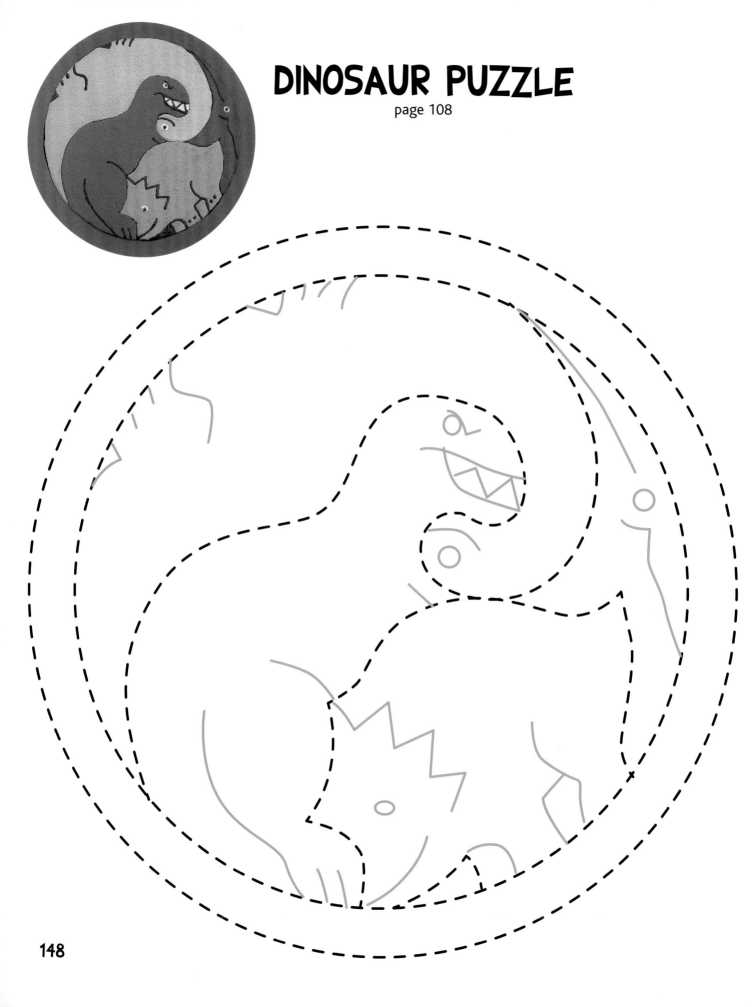

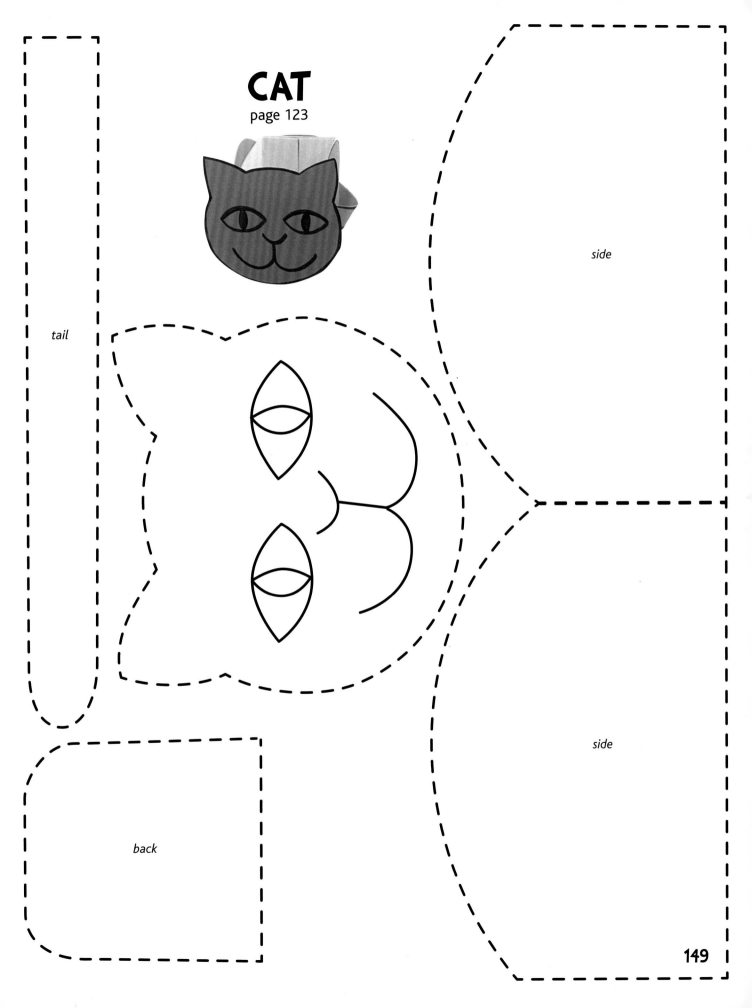

CAT

page 123

side

tail

back

side

149

Materials Index

A

aluminum foil, 13, 33, 48, 94, 134, 138, 142

B

bags
  paper, 21, 138
  plastic, 15, 138
balloons, 120
beads, 28, 34, 36, 119
books, 138
bottle caps and tops, 54, 136
bottles, plastic soda pop, 142
bowls, 18, 68, 114, 138
boxes
  large, 12, 38, 98, 114
  shoe, 96, 112, 140
  small, 88, 96, 106, 119, 122, 132
bristol board, 10, 12, 13, 14, 15, 16, 17, 26, 30, 36, 38, 39, 44, 46, 48, 50, 56, 96, 106, 108, 122, 126, 128, 131, 132
broomsticks, 62
buttons, 34, 56, 64, 88, 90, 104, 114, 136

C

candies, 138
cans, 76
cardboard, 82, 110, 136
  corrugated, 22, 25, 35, 88, 142
cartons
  egg, 20, 82, 122, 131

large ice cream, 13
milk or juice, 118
chairs, 12, 39, 62
chalk, 10, 22, 84, 140
clothespins, 90
containers
  cardboard, 13
  plastic, 46, 82
cornhusks and silk, 70, 72
cornstarch, 18
craft foam, 108
crayons, 21, 64, 128

D

die, 122

E

embroidery floss, 92
envelopes, 126, 138, 140

F

fabric, 10, 24, 26, 64, 72, 84, 96
facecloths, 46
felt, 44, 48, 52, 94, 140
fishing line, 28
flour, 120
food coloring, 18, 82
funnel, 120

G

gimp, 28
glitter, 33
glue, white, 20, 30, 33, 36, 38, 39, 44, 46, 50, 52, 58, 60, 64, 68, 82, 88, 90, 92, 94, 96, 98, 106, 108, 113, 114, 118, 119, 122, 132, 136, 140

googly eyes, 44, 60, 68, 77, 104, 106, 122
grass, 74
grass seed, 68

H

hair bands, 25
hole punch, 12, 14, 17, 20, 22, 25, 36, 48, 50, 84, 106, 110, 114, 119, 134, 140

I

ice-cube trays, 18

J

jars, 76

L

lanyard, 28
leaves
  plastic, 25
  real, 74

M

markers, 12, 46, 48, 52, 54, 56, 58, 60, 62, 64, 106, 108, 122, 131, 136, 142
  fabric, 140
mini-paintings, 113
modeling clay, 74, 77, 88
moss, 80

N

needles, sewing, 44, 104
newspapers, 17, 44